LORI PECKHAM, editor

Guide's Greatest

ANIMAL STORIES

D0793013

REVIEW AND HERALD® PUBLISHING ASSOCIATION
HAGERSTOWN, MD 21740

The Review and Herald Publishing Association publishes biblically
based materials for spiritual, physical, and mental growth and
Christian discipleship.

The author assumes full responsibility for the accuracy of all facts
and quotations as cited in this book.

Unless otherwise noted, Scripture references are from the *Holy
Bible, New International Version*. Copyright © 1973, 1978, 1984,
International Bible Society. Used by permission of Zondervan Bible
Publishers.

This book was
Edited by Lori Peckham
Cover designed by Trent Truman
Cover art by Tim Jessell
Electronic makeup by Shirley M. Bolivar
Typeset: Goudy 13/16

PRINTED IN U.S.A.

10 09 08 07 06   5 4 3 2 1

R&H Cataloging Service
Guide's greatest animal stories,
    compiled and edited by Lori Peckham.

    1. Animals—Stories.   I. Peckham, Lori, 1962-   .

263.2

ISBN 978-0-8280-1944-6

Contents

Also by Lori Peckham:
   Insight Presents More Unforgettable Stories
   Jesus in My Shoes

To order, call **1-800-765-6955.**
   Visit us at **www.reviewandherald.com** for information on other Review and Herald® Products.

   A special thanks to the authors we were unable to locate. If anyone can provide knowledge of their current mailing address, please relay this information to Lori Peckham, in care of the Review and Herald® Publishing Association.

Special Thanks

My profound appreciation and admiration go to the editors of *Guide* magazine—past and present. For more than 50 years they have consistently printed—every single week—powerful, dramatic, life-changing, sometimes humorous, always inspiring stories.

Special thanks to Randy Fishell, the current editor, whose vision for this book—a collection of true, action-packed, spiritual, and classic stories about animals—kept me hunting through 50 years for the very best ones. Special thanks also to Andrea Tymeson, who carefully and cheerfully prepared this manuscript—and who always cries at a good story. (When she told me that some of these stories made her cry, I knew we were on the right track.)

And special thanks to my 3-year-old son, Reef, who came to love some of these stories as much as I did, and who reminded me that a good story speaks to all ages and can change someone's life. His favorite story (chapter 11) inspired him to pour water around his sandbox to create "quicksand," and the backyard will never be the same.

—Lori Peckham

"Thou hast created all things,
and for thy pleasure
they are and were created"
(Revelation 4:11, KJV).

1

Saved by a Crocodile

by Arthur S. Maxwell

Sambo was one of the brightest boys at the mission school, although he was brighter at play than at work.

He had been attending the school for two or three years, but though many of the other boys had given their hearts to Jesus, Sambo had not. He always wanted to "have a good time," and refused to give up some of the bad habits he had brought with him from his village.

Sometimes the people in charge of the mission had thought of sending Sambo home, but again and again they had forgiven him and let him stay on. Someday, they hoped, something might happen that would lead Sambo to love the Lord.

Despite all Sambo's misbehavior, the other boys liked him a great deal, chiefly, perhaps, because he was such a wonderful swimmer. In any sort of race he could leave them all behind, and this made him somewhat of a hero.

One afternoon as they all stood on the bank of the big wide river where they went to bathe, one of the boys dared Sambo to swim clear across to the other side and back again.

No one had ever done it before. It was against the rules. Because of the current and the crocodiles, the boys were supposed to stay in their own quiet pool.

But now, as Sambo hesitated, they all began to tease him.

"You're afraid," one said.

"I'm not," declared Sambo.

"You couldn't swim that far," said another.

"I could," said Sambo.

"Then why don't you do it?" asked a third.

"Maybe I will," said Sambo. "Maybe I will."

But when he did not go in immediately, they taunted him some more.

"Let's see you do it!" they cried. "We'll count and see how long you take."

"All right," said Sambo. "I'll try."

"Watch the crocodiles!" cried someone as Sambo slipped into the water.

"Don't worry about the crocs," he replied. "I can swim faster than they can."

And he was off. With powerful strokes he worked upriver against the current, then over toward the middle. While the others held their breath at the daring feat, Sambo drew nearer and nearer to the opposite bank.

At last he stopped swimming and began to walk out of the water. At this all the boys clapped their hands and shouted, "Well done, Sambo! Well done!"

For a while Sambo sat on the bank getting his breath for the return trip. Finally, as the others watched and shouted to him, he entered the water and began the long swim back.

Then it happened.

Sambo had not been in the water more than two or three minutes when one of the boys saw a long, low shape moving toward him. It was like a floating tree trunk, but with hard, cruel eyes.

"A crocodile!" the boy cried.

Then they all saw it, and with one accord they yelled, "Look out, Sambo! There's a crocodile right behind you!"

Sambo heard the warning and, looking around, saw the terrible beast coming straight toward him.

He almost leaped out of the water. Never in his life had he swum so fast. Always he had thought he could outswim a crocodile. But could he? Could he?

Terrified, the others watched the grim race.

For a little while it looked as though Sambo might win. With a great burst of speed he pulled ahead. But no boy alive could keep up such a pace.

Gradually the distance narrowed, and the crocodile got nearer and nearer.

Suddenly there was a splash, a snap, and poor Sambo disappeared.

With wild cries of fear and sorrow the boys rushed back to the mission.

But when the mission director heard the story, he ordered search parties out at once. "Crocodiles," he explained, "do not eat their prey as soon as they catch it, but bury it until they are ready for their meal. There is just one chance in a hundred that Sambo might still be alive."

So the search parties started out, combing every yard of both banks of the river, upstream and down.

Meanwhile, Sambo, dragged under the water, had lost consciousness. Then, in a narrow inlet hidden by bushes, the crocodile had covered him with mud and sticks and stones, fortunately leaving his head above water.

When consciousness returned, Sambo awoke to find himself in a crocodile's lair! He was ready to scream with fear. But at that very moment he remembered something he had been taught in the mission school.

He thought about Jesus.

"Jesus!" he cried. "Save me from the crocodile! Please save me from the crocodile, and I will be your boy always."

Even as he cried out he heard the tramp of feet. Soon he was looking up into the faces of some of the people from the mission, who were searching for him. Quickly they tore away the sticks and rocks, put Sambo on a stretcher, and carried him back to the mission hospital.

Today Sambo walks on crutches because of what the crocodile did to his leg. But he doesn't seem to mind. There's a joy on his face, and he's one of the finest Christians you could wish to meet.

2

Panther in the Pines

by Gwendolen Lampshire Hayden

Ma, how long will you be gone?" Melinda asked. She watched her mother gather up medicines and bandages and pack them in a bag.

"I don't know, dear," Mrs. Brown replied. "Neighbor Belshaw said his boy was hurt pretty bad when his horse threw him."

Mrs. Brown paused to look at her oldest daughter. "From the looks of the sky this afternoon, I think we're due for a change of weather. It might be a good idea for Zebulun to tie Buttercup in the milk shed. Then if a storm does blow up, he can milk her without having to go to the corral. It doesn't pay to take any chances when danger may be lurking near."

"We'll be all right, Ma," Melinda said with a shaky little laugh. "After all, this isn't the first time we've had to stay alone while you were taking care of some sick neighbor. But for some reason I just feel chills running up and down my back as I think about our staying alone tonight. I guess it's because the sky looks so stormy and the wind's begun to howl. I wish Pa'd get home from Canyon City this evening."

"I wish so too, darling." Ma put her arm around Melinda and kissed her cheek. "But you know it takes almost a week for him to make that long trip each fall for our winter supplies."

Melinda opened the cabin door, and Zebulun blew inside with a blast of wind. "Cayuse is all saddled up," he gasped. "You'd better get started, Ma. It looks like a storm for sure."

Mrs. Brown mounted Cayuse, then said, "Be sure to keep the fire going, son, and get the milking done early so you don't have to go outside after dark. Read baby sister her Bible story before bedtime, and hear her say her prayers, Melinda. Now I must hurry. Dark closes in fast in these high mountains."

Melinda and Zebulun stood in the doorway and watched until Mother's Indian pony turned the bend along the willow-bordered creek. Then they hurried into the stout little cabin, and Melinda shut and latched the door.

"There's not much use bolting the door," Zebulun said. "I've still got the milking to do." He hurried to the small front window and peered out at the scudding storm clouds. "It's going to get dark awfully fast.

I think I'll grab the pail and milk old Buttercup right now, even if it is a little early."

"That's a good idea," Melinda nodded. "Before you go out, will you please build up the fire? Dolly should wake up before long, and I want the room to be nice and warm. Then maybe you'd better bring in that last big load of wood. That way you won't have to go outside after dark, especially when we know there are panthers near. Did you hear that one wailing last night? He sounded as though he might be right behind the cabin and up on Sagebrush Ridge."

"Did I hear him!" Zebulun exclaimed. "I guess that's one reason I'm ready to milk early tonight."

"Belshaw told us there's a wounded one, and they're especially dangerous," Melinda said, her cheeks pink from the warmth of the fireplace. "Oh! Dolly's waking up."

Zebulun took the shining tin milk pail and hurried out into the afternoon's fading light. Quickly he looked down the narrow mountain canyon for a view of Buttercup's smooth red-and-white sides. But all he saw were the swaying pine trees along the mountain creek that dashed past the cabin and wandered down the steep mountain.

"Buttercup, O Buttercup," he called. He cupped his strong, weather-beaten hands around his mouth and shouted first in one direction and then in another.

But though he listened carefully for the gentle

cow's answering moo, he heard no sound but the faint echo of his own words.

"I wonder if that pesky critter's wandered down by the irrigation ditch I've been digging," he muttered to himself. "She followed me there yesterday, and she may have seen me digging in that ditch again today. I never saw such a cow. She follows us around just like a dog. Well, I'll have to go and bring her home. It's too far away for her to hear my voice. Maybe it's a good thing I have to go down there, though, because I forgot to bring my shovel home with me."

Zebulun turned to the right and ran down the narrow mountain trail that led to the new irrigation ditch he had been digging in preparation for watering early spring crops. As he hurried along he was conscious of the coldness of the rising wind that tugged at his coat. He caught his breath as he emerged from the pine trees and looked eagerly toward the deep ditch, where he hoped to find the family cow.

His face clouded with disappointment. "She's not here," he sighed. "Well, I better pick up that shovel I left here this morning. Whew! I don't know when I've been so short of breath. Guess I hurried along at a pretty fast rate. I think I'll sit down in that ditch out of the wind and rest a minute before starting back."

Zebulun never knew just how long he sat there before he heard the sudden dull thud near him. He never knew when he first turned his sleepy gaze toward the right. But he always remembered the horrible fear that gripped him as he stared straight into the savage yellow eyes of the snarling creature that crouched nearby. He always remembered the sickening terror that seemed to freeze the very blood in his veins as the animal's roar trembled in the cold air and seemed to hang threateningly overhead.

A panther! It's the wounded panther. And it's getting ready to spring. What will I do? Zebulun felt his thoughts whirl dizzily around and around.

He felt stunned by the suddenness of the beast's appearance and by the overwhelming certainty that within seconds the enraged animal would attack. He shuddered as he looked at the rippling back muscles bunched ready to spring and at the cruel, rending claws eager to spill his blood.

"What shall I do? What can I do?" he moaned to himself. His thoughts flew across the intervening pathway to the little cabin he had left a short time before. His eyes seemed to pierce the distance and look in through the rough walls to his two sisters waiting for his return.

When I don't come back, Melinda will begin looking for me, he thought, almost sick with the fear that gripped him. *She won't know what's happened to me. She'll have to leave the baby alone while she searches. She'll start out, and the panther will be waiting somewhere along the trail for her, too. Then maybe Dolly will open the cabin door. Even if the panther doesn't kill her, the cold air will. Oh, dear God, help me. Help me think of some way to spare our lives.*

Zebulun's thoughts spun as his eyes roved here and there in search of some weapon of defense. Just as his frantic gaze fell upon the abandoned shovel lying within arm's length, he heard the fierce roar of the mountain lion as it sprang forward. He felt his hand grasp the shovel's cold handle. Then he was amazed to find himself scrambling up the side of the ditch, away from the beast's rushing attack. He whirled just in time to see the animal's snarling leap. Quickly he struck forward with the shovel's shining blade.

Wham!

He staggered from the tremendous impact of steel against living flesh. His ears throbbed from the roar that shattered the air and sent it into wildly flying echoes.

Wham!

So great was the force of his second direct hit upon the leaping panther that his muscles ached as though he had been beaten.

He's cringing, Zebulun thought, panting with his desperate exertion. *He—he's resting a minute too. Look at the blood running down his head from that long cut. Well, I know I've got to rest. I don't know how much longer I can hold him off.* As he saw the panther's muscles tighten for another leap, he raised the shovel over his head and breathed a quick, silent prayer.

Zebulun never forgot the tremendous strength that surged through his tired arms just as the panther leaped straight for his throat. He never forgot the power that seemed to grip his own arms and bring the shovel straight down on the mountain lion's head. He never forgot the thrill that shook him as the wounded beast staggered, almost fell, and then turned and ran straight toward the river.

Zebulun took only one look in the direction of the fleeing panther. Then, clutching the shovel as though it were as light as straw, he sped back up the mountain trail.

He flung open the door of the cabin and stopped short, gasping painfully for breath. Not until that moment did he feel any lack of the strength that had so miraculously sustained him. But now that he was safe within the shelter of the four walls, he felt so weak that he could scarcely stand. He looked at the gleaming kerosene lamp and wondered dully why its light seemed to fade out, in and out. He wondered why his sister's voice sounded so far away. And then for the first time in his life he fainted.

"What—where am I?" he gasped. He tried to sit up, but collapsed instead on the bed. "I—where's Buttercup? And the panther—did it—"

"Hush now," he heard Melinda reply. "Buttercup's safe in the milking shed. Shortly after you left she wandered in of her own free will, and I milked her. I finished up the chores while you were gone. Something just seemed to tell me to hurry, hurry, hurry and get everything done. I didn't know why I felt so nervous and uneasy. But all the time I kept thinking of you and wondering if you were all right. You must have met that wounded mountain lion that the hunters have been trailing for the past several days. Here now, drink this cup of hot broth. Then you can tell me what happened."

Far into the night Zebulun and Melinda sat beside the warmth of the fire in the big stone fireplace. Outside the wind moaned around the corners of the rough cabin. They shivered as now and then above its eerie crescendo they heard the sound of a panther crying in the dark night.

"Listen!" whispered Melinda. "Do you hear that? It must be the wounded beast that attacked you this afternoon. Oh, Zeb! How thankful I am that your life has been spared. You saved my life, too. I'd surely have started looking for you after a while and perhaps . . ."

Her voice trailed away into a frightened silence. But she looked up as Zebulun put his big brown hand over hers.

"We must never forget, Melinda, that God really does answer our prayers. I could never have fought that panther with my own strength."

3

Billy, the Terrible-tempered Goat

by Maryane G. Myers

He was the finest goat in 10 states, Alice decided as she leaned across the droopy wire fence. Billy's eyes were as bright as new tin cans, and his chin whiskers flapped as delightfully as a white sock on the clothesline on a breezy day. Yes, indeed, he was the finest goat in 10 states—maybe 48, for that matter.

However, there was one thing wrong with him, she had to admit. Billy had a terrible temper.

"You were as tame as a kitten when you were small, but Bob and Joe have teased you until you even look mean," she told the family pet.

The goat stopped chewing on a paper carton, turned his back, and nibbled on the rope that tied him.

"Perhaps I teased a bit too," Alice confessed. "Never as severely as the boys, though. Yet I can't understand why Mother has forbidden me to play with you. Maybe she thinks you're too rough. As if a girl couldn't handle a goat!"

She laughed, walked to the gate, and went inside. "With my brothers away and Mother in the house, I think this would be a good time to ride a goat."

Billy looked up and shook his head as if to say, "That's what you think."

"I'm not afraid of your horns—that is, not as long as you're tied to the oak tree," Alice exclaimed. "You can't go far."

The goat, apparently disinterested, went back to nibbling on the rope.

Alice advanced bravely and patted Billy on the head. He gave his ears a little shake and continued to look about for something to eat, as if he hadn't already had enough breakfast for two goats his size.

Slowly, and a bit apprehensively, Alice climbed aboard his sturdy white back. "Giddap, Billy!" She gave him a sharp slap to get him started. She had seen him take her brothers for short trots around the tree, and expected the same. "Here we go!" she urged, but Billy still did not go.

She administered another sharper slap on his side to arouse him. It was like lighting $50 worth of fireworks all at one time. Billy bucked like a bronco, fought the ground like a panther, and steamed like an engine—all of which produced a scene of wild rage and sent Alice flying over his head in a couple somersaults. Then he jumped around frantically on a rampage.

Greatly shaken but uninjured, Alice picked herself up out of the dust and dived for the gate. "Wow!" she exclaimed. "That was a close call."

But one backward glance at Billy told her that her troubles had only started. The rope that had tied him to the tree had snapped in two. He was free, and pawing the air like a wild animal.

Alice was too frightened to scream or think. She swallowed a mouthful of air and ran as fast as she could toward the house. Without looking back, she knew that Billy had leaped the fence and was in close pursuit. His hoofs seemed to thunder at her heels.

Frantically she raced toward the back door. "Mother!" she cried. But she did not have time to get inside. Billy was too close for that.

So she ran around the house. "Mother, open the door!" she called.

By that time her mother was at the door, holding it open. However, the goat's horns were too close to permit her to safely step inside.

Again she raced around the house, almost out of breath. Again the animal lunged forward just as she attempted to run inside.

The length and breadth of the house had never seemed so great before. Alice was breathing hard as she started around the third time. She almost stumbled on a clump of flowers just as she reached the door again. With an extra spurt of energy, she bounded inside the house and leaned breathlessly against the closed door. Then with a moan she pointed to the kitchen windows. The fight was not over.

Billy, trembling and snorting, was glaring in the windows. For a moment he dashed away, butted against the door, and then came back to the windows.

"Mother," Alice gasped, "he's going to try to get through the window."

Mother shook her head. "Billy can't get in. The windowpanes are too small."

"One is broken and hasn't been replaced," Alice reminded her. Then she had an idea. "Mother, do you mind if I use our old mirror for a windowpane? If Billy sees himself, he may decide to go away."

"That's a good idea," said Mother, hurrying to the pantry, where the old mirror was kept on a high shelf. "Here it is. Do you want to take it to the window?"

"Yes," said Alice. "He gave me a scare, and now I'm going to teach him a lesson. He's never seen himself before."

The animal was prancing up and down outside, butting against the house and making a fearful racket. Alice slipped the mirror into the opening of the broken window, behind the screen wire.

Suddenly the goat saw it. He jumped backward.

Then, instead of making a dive for the side of the house, he ran straight for the mirror, breaking through the wire mesh and shattering the glass.

It was a cut, stunned, and bewildered goat that disentangled his head and horns from the window frame. He stood there shaking himself, then turned and ran as fast as he could back to the shelter of the oak tree.

Alice and Mother stood at the back door watching him go.

"Mother, I'm so sorry for disobeying you," Alice said.

Mother put her arms around her. "You could have been killed."

Alice thought of a Bible text she had recently learned: "Do not make friends with a hot-tempered man, do not associate with one easily angered" (Proverbs 22:24). It could also apply to a goat, she decided. Bad temper means trouble in people or beasts.

"You have my promise that I will leave Billy alone," she told her mother. "He may look like the finest goat in 10 states, but that awful temper spoils it all." Then she added to herself, "I think I'll start watching my own temper, or I may not like what I see when I look into a mirror someday."

4

The Scoffer Silenced

by Etta B. Degering

I t was February 1942. The dense fog at Leuchars Air Base in Scotland had lifted at last. Reconnaissance planes could again take to the air.

Sergeant Davidson, in charge of Operation Pigeon, stepped outside his billet and breathed in gulps of the clear salt air. He noticed the beach smells of kelp and fish mingled with the air-base smells of gasoline and oil. He heard the shrill call of gulls and the roar of planes warming up.

Sergeant Davidson was on his way to check the homing pigeons that had just been brought in from Broughty Ferry, seven miles away. Owners of racing pigeons lent birds to the RAF (Royal Air Force) every other week for a period of 48 hours. Sergeant Davidson made a record of the numbers the pigeons wore on their leg rings, and then checked them out to the airplanes by twos in two-bird wicker baskets.

Number 1, wrote Sergeant Davidson. The number intrigued him. It had the sound of a blue ribbon—a first prize. Was this pigeon something special? Not to look at, he decided. She was just a smoky blue chequer hen, a little larger than the average, perhaps, but with no special markings.

The blue pigeon cocked her head to one side, and her large red eyes stared at the man. "Cu-r-r-oo," she said and sidestepped toward the divider that separated her from her flying mate, a little red hen.

Sergeant Davidson assigned the pair to plane M *for Mother*.

The checking finished, Sergeant Davidson picked up a basket containing a pure white hen and a small runty one. Then he hurried toward the hangar where he was supposed to explain to the air crews how to handle the pigeons—how to make out the SOS form that the birds wore in special plastic capsules on their legs, and how to release them in case of emergency.

Usually the men listened interestedly to his lectures, but once in a while some skeptic who didn't believe in "pigeon nonsense" gave him a bad time. Today proved to be one of those days. A young wireless operator with a pencil-fine mustache, sharp features, and a still sharper wit had a lot of fun scoffing at the instructor.

As a climax to his brief lecture, Sergeant

Davidson called for volunteers to fill out the SOS form and release the birds. The pigeon owners were told to be on the lookout for them.

That's when things went from bad to worse. The runty hen, scared half to death from so much handling, flew back inside the building instead of taking off for her loft, and she sought refuge on a girder near the roof, where no one could reach her. The hangar fairly exploded with hoots and laughter.

When order was restored, the white hen was released. She redeemed the honor of her feathered clan by making a neat takeoff and flying in a straight line the seven miles to her loft in Broughty Ferry. In 10 minutes a telephone call announced her arrival.

After his lecture, Sergeant Davidson, feeling pretty low, doggedly went about the day's routine. The sun shone through and burned off the remaining fog. The afternoon was sunny, and the evening gave promise of a frosty, clear, moonlit night.

One by one the reconnaissance planes returned, and the pigeons were collected and fed. Finally only one pair was left to be accounted for—the birds booked out to M *for Mother*. Inquiry at the signal office revealed the plane overdue, and it was hoped that it had landed safely at some other station. But later in the evening an official report confirmed that aircraft M was missing.

Sergeant Davidson called the owners of the blue

chequer hen and the red hen—Messrs. Ross and Norrie, outstanding long-distance racers of pigeons.

"No, neither bird has come home," the men said. They would keep watch.

The birds had had extensive training, especially Number 1, the blue hen. She had flown from points north and south along the coast of Scotland. She had also been released from various types of aircraft over the North Sea. But Mr. Ross didn't expect either bird to come in now until morning. They were not night fliers. If they had made the coast by dusk, they would roost in some tree until daylight.

It was a long night. Searching planes were dispatched in the general direction from which the last faint radio message from M *for Mother* had been received. An early morning call to Mr. Ross revealed that the homers had not returned. During breakfast, while three more planes were warming up to join the search, a pilot came running to Sergeant Davidson's quarters.

"Sarge, Sarge, one of those birds is home!"

This was news! The planes were held. Sergeant Davidson rushed to a telephone. Soon Mr. Ross was on the line. "Yes, the blue hen trapped in."

"What time?"

"I'd say about 8:25. She wasn't there when I left the loft after feeding, but as I was leaving for work, I saw her on the trap."

"You say she had no message?"

"No, only the regular SOS form in the tube."

"What is her condition?"

"Oh, she has had a good fly, but she could have gone on for some time. The ends of her flight and tail feathers look darker than the rest, as if they might have been in the sea."

"Dunked, no doubt, when the plane ditched," said the sergeant.

Quickly calculating from the information received—the pigeon's flying speed, her loss of weight, the weather, and the fact that she was not a night flier and must have roosted about 40 miles away to fly home an hour after dawn—Sergeant Davidson informed the waiting planes: "It looks as though the bird was flying about four hours. That would mean she had covered from 120 to 140 miles."

The three planes roared off. But they were back in a short time. Fearing that the planes had returned because fog had hindered further search, Sergeant Davidson called the signal officers. "What's up? Too much pea soup?"

"Oh, haven't you heard? After your report the search planes were told to make a circle of a 120- to 140-mile radius, and they found the lifeboat of M *for Mother* in about 20 minutes."

"The crew OK?"

"So far as I know. An aircraft is circling them

now, and Air-Sea Rescue launches are on their way to pick them up."

Sergeant Davidson's morale soared. The pigeon service had paid off! He was eager to get the full report, but it was necessary to wait a few days. The crew of M *for Mother* was taken to the nearest hospital to recuperate from exposure. They had been adrift 21 hours in the bitterly cold February weather.

When the rescued men returned to Leuchars Air Base, Sergeant Davidson called on them. First he went to see the wireless operator, but he was not in his billet. He then visited the pilot and navigator, who gave him the details of their harrowing experience. He took notes as they talked.

The plane's port engine had caught fire. The crew knew they were in for a ditching—and soon. The navigator took a quick reading of their position, and the wireless operator screwed down his distress signal.

Then the crash!

The plane drifted half submerged only a few minutes. As the pigeon basket floated past the wireless operator in the rear hatch, he tossed it into the sea, where it remained afloat with its struggling birds. The men barely got away from the plane before it sank.

The dinghy broke loose, and two of the men had to swim for it. They then rowed in it to pick up the pigeons and put their training into practice.

"You can't know, Sarge, without being there,"

said the navigator, "how much those pigeons meant to us."

When the pigeon basket was lifted from the water, the door to one compartment fell open, and the blue hen made a quick takeoff—in the right direction, but without any message. The little red hen was nearly drowned. Her end of the basket had floated almost entirely underwater. The men dried her and filled out the SOS form. After much coaxing, she too took off, but evidently she never reached home.

The story was finished. Telling it made the men sober. Sergeant Davidson thanked them and congratulated them on their escape. They in turn praised him for his work in Operation Pigeon.

Sergeant Davidson folded his notes, put them in his pocket, and went to lunch. While he was eating, someone touched him on the shoulder, and a voice said, "I hear you were looking for me."

Sergeant Davidson turned around. He stared. It couldn't be—but it was. It was the scoffer with the fine-pointed mustache.

"Were you the wireless operator on M?" he asked.

"None other."

"Well, how about that! It had to be you!" said Sergeant Davidson.

And then the wireless operator of M *for Mother* erased all former joking by one humble, sincere statement: "That pigeon, Sarge—she saved our lives."

A dinner was given in the officers' mess for the crew of M *for Mother* and their squadron. Mr. Ross and Pigeon Number 1 were honored guests. As a special feature, the smoky blue hen, which up to this time had been nameless, was christened Winkie. Mr. Ross was presented with a bronze plaque depicting a pigeon flying over the sea. And the plastic capsule with its SOS form, which Winkie carried on her perilous flight, was given to Sergeant Davidson for a keepsake.

Winkie was honorably retired from flight service. She became the chief attraction at charity functions for orphans up and down the country and seemed to like the attention and life of a hero.

5

Darlene Hangs Up Her Spurs

by Moeita M. Burch

O h, Uncle Bill, could I have it?" Darlene begged.

"I suppose so. That foal is of no use to me." The man was obviously annoyed as he looked at the little filly that had just been born. Her front toes turned in, and he knew she would always be in danger of tripping over them when she walked.

The little pigeon-toed animal nuzzled Darlene's arm, while the Arabian mare, Sharika, breathed upon her baby with a proud mother's love.

"Then she's mine!" Darlene cried. "And I'll call her Little Midge. I can never thank you enough!"

"I hope you can get some use of her," Uncle Bill said. "She'll never sell, you know."

"*Sell?* Who'd do that? I'll never sell Little Midge, *never!* She's going to be my cow pony."

"Humph," her uncle grunted. "She's more likely to fall down and break her neck."

Darlene could hardly wait until Midge was weaned. Her uncle Bill owned a ranch in Wyoming, where he bred and sold polo ponies, while Darlene's father, a cattle herder, lived on an adjoining spread. There were always plenty of horses to use, but Darlene had longed for a little foal of her own to love and train. Now she had one.

When Midge was 2 years old, she was ready to be ridden. Patience and kindness had made her very gentle, and she learned readily how to dodge in and out of the brush after an uncooperative steer. She wasn't trained as a cutting horse because of her front feet, but the slightly turned-in hoofs never stumbled as Uncle Bill had predicted. She could sit on her haunches and slide down an embankment with the best of the horses, and her never-tiring running walk delighted Darlene. To her, the filly was worth a million dollars.

Next to Midge, Darlene's pride was a pair of silver-mounted spurs, a birthday gift from Uncle Bill.

"What do you want with those sharp things?" her mother said. "It's mean to jab spurs into a horse's sides."

"Oh, Mom," Darlene argued, "I never jab Midge. I barely touch her with the spurs."

"Then why do you use them?"

"They look so pretty on my boots," Darlene confessed.

Mother shook her head. "Vanity, vanity."

Then one day, in spite of Darlene's intentions, she did use those spurs. It was the day before Dad planned to sell the prime steers. Darlene overheard him talking to one of the ranch hands. "It's possible that those three steers are on Hogback Ridge. We need them to make up the load."

"Oh, Dad!" Darlene cried. "Please let Midge and I go hunt them."

Father hesitated. "That's a long ride for a girl."

"I'm not a baby," Darlene argued, "and Midge is plenty fast. I'll take Dingo to locate them, and we'll do the rest. Please, Dad. I've been aching all week for a nice long ride."

"Very well," he consented. "But watch out for a storm. I don't like those black clouds. I'd rather be short a dozen steers than have my girl hurt."

"Oh, Dad, I know Wyoming squalls as well as you do, and I have no desire to be caught in one."

Darlene hurried to get Midge ready, then ran to the house for her cherished spurs. Mother came in as she was buckling the second one on.

"It would never do to forget those ornaments," she teased. "Your boots wouldn't look right without them."

"No, they wouldn't," Darlene agreed merrily.

"Take your slicker," Father said. "Wait, and I'll tie it behind your saddle. I still don't like that sky."

"Thanks, Dad. We'll be OK," Darlene assured him.

Heading Midge toward the hills, Darlene whistled to Dingo, the sharp-eared collie that came on a run, eager to be of service. Midge fell into her speedy, running walk, and every so often Darlene lifted her into an easy lope as they crossed the level valley. "We have a long way to go, and Dad is scared of the weather," she said, patting the filly's glossy neck.

They covered the miles in record time, and soon they were in the brush and timber of Hogback Ridge. Well-trained Dingo knew his job, and off he scouted for the missing steers. Darlene glanced again at the sky. Off in the distance she saw a black sheet of cloud with great streaks running down to the earth.

"I hope that downpour doesn't catch up with us," Darlene told Midge.

Where could those ornery steers be? Dingo had worked the entire ridge and now was back with lolling tongue and apologetic eyes that seemed to say, "I did my best, but there aren't any cattle here."

Just then a few big drops of rain splashed on Darlene's hat, and Midge fidgeted nervously. Suddenly the leaden sky opened and a hard, driving rain pelted down on the trio. Darlene's hands were so cold that she had difficulty untying her slicker, but once enveloped in its folds, she felt better.

I guess we'd better head for home, she thought. *Those steers aren't here, or Dingo would've found them.* "Come on, Dingo," she called. "I know you tried hard. Maybe you can find them nearer home."

Midge trotted among the trees, shaking her head in the open stretches as the huge drops of rain hammered on her ears. "Poor Midge; this is awful," Darlene said, "and it's a long way to the ranch."

She glanced at her watch and was surprised to see that it was much later than she had thought. It would soon be dark and hard to find the way in the heavy timber of the ridge. Even in the valley it would be difficult to see landmarks; so she decided to follow the gulch instead.

A creek had flowed through it decades ago, but new channels had diverted the water, and the gully had been dry for a long time. Its sides were high, and Darlene knew she couldn't possibly get lost, as the gulch ended not too far from their first meadow. It was rocky, but Midge was surefooted and wouldn't fall.

They were forging ahead at a steady gait when the filly suddenly turned and lunged up the embankment.

"I know it's rocky, Midge, but you have good shoes, and there's no excuse for this kind of behavior. I have a reason for staying in the gulch." Darlene neck-reined the horse sharply, and Midge reluctantly slid back down the bank.

The rain had slackened now, but they hadn't gone 20 yards farther when Midge scrambled out of the gulch again.

"What ails you, Midge?" Darlene scolded. "You

need a lesson in obedience." She reined the filly down again and spurred her sharply.

Midge obeyed, but 10 feet later she lunged wildly up the bank for the third time. Darlene was angry now. "You stubborn little beast!" she cried. "I'll show you who's boss."

She yanked on the reins, but Midge had the bit in her teeth and refused to budge. Then the silver-mounted spurs went into action, and the sharp rowels bit deep. Still the filly refused to obey the signals.

In desperation, Darlene scraped the spurs along Midge's sides from flank to shoulder and back again. *This is one time that my spurs are useful as well as ornamental*, she thought.

Midge sprang to the edge of the bank and stopped short. It was as if she were trying to say, "Are you sure you want to go this way?"

An odd noise caught Darlene's attention, and she stared into the gulch. A swirl of muddy water was churning down the creek bed and getting deeper every minute. As she watched in fascination, great boulders began rushing and grinding along, followed by logs, brush, and debris.

All at once Darlene thought of what her spurs had done. She slid out of the saddle, threw her arms around Midge's neck, and burst into tears. "Oh, Midge, Midge, you saved my life. God told you that flood was coming," she sobbed. In remorse she rubbed her fingers along the filly's side and drew them away, sticky with blood. She cried anew at the sight, and caressed Midge's brown face.

The pony nuzzled her as if to say, "I forgive you. You didn't understand."

Darlene bent and unbuckled each spur as fast as she could. Then she hung them over the saddle horn and remounted. It was getting dark, but Midge trotted swiftly and unerringly through the timber until finally they reached the broad valley. Midge seemed to know exactly where to go, so Darlene gave her free rein, and before she realized it they were home.

Darlene's first task was to bathe and salve those awful spur wounds. Then she retired the silver-mounted spurs to the wall above her saddle.

That evening Darlene said to her mother, "How did Midge know the gulch was going to flood? The creek bed was as dry as a bone. An angel must have guided her. I felt like Balaam when he beat his donkey. Only the donkey was made to talk, but poor Midge couldn't say a word."

"It seems that to make up for their lack of speech, God has given animals an extra amount of instinct," Mother said. And she added, "I'm glad those spurs are on the wall instead of on your boots."

"So am I," Darlene agreed.

And that is where they remained from then on.

6

The Faithful Friend

by Kay Warwick

Oh, Bert, where do you suppose Sammy could be?" Ellen leaned her head on her hand and looked very sad.

Her young husband wanted to tell her not to worry, that he was sure her puppy would be found; but in all truthfulness, he did not feel he could. For when a small dog has been missing for six days in Africa, that usually means it has been killed by another animal or caught in a trap and starved to death.

"I know you miss Sammy, Ellen, but I'm afraid there's no hope for him now." Bert put his hand over his wife's hand. He knew it was lonesome for Ellen, living here in this rough construction camp with no other young people around.

"At least you've still got Blackie for company!"

Bert grinned as a large black crow flew up and landed on the windowsill near them.

Ellen had to laugh. "He's such a scamp, always getting into something. Bert, if you hadn't found him after his wing was broken, I'm sure he'd be dead by now. And I know he misses Sammy, too. They were great friends."

Blackie cocked his head to one side as though he knew his masters were discussing him. Then with a flash of his wings he flew into the kitchen and landed beside his dish of food.

The young engineer watched the crow pick at his meal; then he frowned. "Well, what on earth's the matter with him now?"

Blackie had taken the largest piece of bread into his beak and was flying out the window with it.

Ellen shrugged. "I don't know. He's been doing that lately. Do you suppose he's got a nest or a hidey-hole in a tree and puts food there for later?"

Bert shook his head. "I don't think so. Crows and magpies steal shiny things sometimes and hide them that way, but not food. Tonight at supper let's watch Blackie and see if we can follow him. He's got my curiosity stirred up!"

That evening the young couple watched, and their crow behaved in exactly the same way. He took a bit of food in his beak, flew off, and returned a short time later to fetch another piece. The second time this happened Bert and Ellen were ready and followed him. He was carrying a prize piece of meat.

"H'mmm, I believe that rascal knows we're following him. At least he's surely making it easy for us!" Bert exclaimed.

Ellen saved her breath and hurried after her husband, keeping her eyes on the crow.

Staying just ahead of the young couple, the crow seemed to be heading for a small clump of bushes at the entrance of a ravine. When he reached the spot, he disappeared into the thick bush.

Bert gave a peculiar whistle that the crow always answered, but this time the answer was different. Instead of the hoarse, strident caw of the crow, there came a pleading whimper.

Ellen stopped stock-still. "Oh, Bert!" she exclaimed hopefully. "It couldn't be—or could it?"

Bert shot her a quick, incredulous glance. "Now, honey," he said, "don't get your hopes up." But already he was pushing his way into the tangle of brush.

Bert came upon a sight that staggered him. There in a little clearing lay their small puppy, Sammy. He was wriggling and whimpering ecstatically at the sight of them.

"Oh, Bert, he's been caught in a trap!" Ellen cried, right at his heels.

The young couple knelt beside him, and Bert

carefully freed the puppy from the snare. Blackie sat beside them on the ground, occasionally cawing at them. The small piece of meat he had been carrying lay in front of him.

"Do you know what that rascal's been doing, Ellen?" Bert exclaimed as he put the freed puppy into his wife's arms.

"I—I can hardly believe it. Do you mean Blackie's been bringing food to Sammy all these days?"

"That's the only possible answer. You can see for yourself that Sammy is in perfect health; without Blackie he would have starved to death in these six days."

Bert held out his hand, and Blackie hopped onto his wrist. He cocked his head to one side and cawed as if to ask, "Aren't I a smart one?"

Bert laughed at him, then remarked thoughtfully, "I've read somewhere that crows sometimes form unusual friendships and when put to the test are courageous and faithful allies."

7

Dick's Pet

by Reva I. Smith

D ick wanted one thing—a pet.

Oh, there was old Rover, the farm dog that had come with the farm when Dad bought it. But he wasn't Dick's own, and he lived outside. He was a working dog and brought the cows home from pasture every night. There were two or three cats, but they too lived outdoors, making their own living by keeping down the mice in the barns.

Actually, what Dick *really* wanted was a pet lamb. Just why Dick thought a lamb would make a better pet than the dog and the cats, he couldn't have told you. Perhaps it was because of the appealing pictures of lambs in his Bible books, or maybe it was the softness of their wool or their trusting, gentle eyes.

One afternoon Dad came upon Dick sitting by the creek that ran through the pasture. "Well, Dick," he said, "I think maybe I'll have some good news for you soon."

Dick looked at his father expectantly. "What is it, Dad? Can't you tell me now?"

"Well, I could tell you now, but you can't have it yet."

"Have what?" begged Dick. "What can't I have? Is it a lamb?"

"Oh, now, don't get so excited!" cautioned Dad. "You'll only be disappointed. No, it's not a lamb . . . "

Dick's smile faded.

Dad went on. "But it is a pet, or it will be, maybe. You know our old fat pig, Petunia? When she has her babies, how would you like to keep one for a pet?"

"A pig?" Dick looked a little doubtful. But baby pigs were rather cute, he decided. "Sure, Dad," he said. "If I kept it really clean all the time, it might not be too bad."

The more he thought about it, the more the idea appealed to him. Finally the day came when the six tiny piglets were born. Dick held his nose each time he went to look at them. He soon picked out one to be his own, and in a few weeks he had his long-awaited pet, which he named Pansy.

For a little while he almost forgot he had wanted a lamb. But he was never allowed to bring the piglet into the house. In fact, no one even wanted *him* in the house after he had been playing with Pansy!

Dick soon realized that if he was to make a real pet of Pansy, he was going to have to make some changes—in Pansy, that is! Cunning and lovable as she might be, she still had some rather uncouth habits, such as rolling in mud (the stickier the better) and slurping up garbage in the most disgusting manner. More than once she had gotten Dick into trouble by muddying up his clothes.

Dick decided to put Pansy Pig through a course in cleanliness and manners. Then perhaps she would turn into a pet he could really enjoy, and maybe he could even bring her into the house now and then. So far his mother hadn't allowed him to bring Pansy any closer than the screen door on the back porch.

One Sunday afternoon when Mother was entertaining company, Dick decided to begin his pig-cleaning campaign. He dragged a washtub out to the backyard and filled it with water. He took a bunch of rags from his mother's rag bag and got a bar of her laundry soap. Then he buttered a crust of bread to entice Pansy over to the washtub. It worked.

But getting Pansy into the tub was somewhat of a problem, and keeping her in it was even more of a problem! Pansy didn't mind water, even cold water, just as long as it had lots of dirt in it—enough dirt to turn it into mud.

But Dick's determination was equal to Pansy's, and since he weighed at least six times as much as

Pansy, he won out. Soon he had his pet washed and dried and ready for "decorating."

"Now, you stay right here!" Dick commanded. "I'll be right back. I've got to find something!" He ran into the house and up the stairs into his sister's bedroom, muttering, "If that Pansy gets dirty . . . Oh, I should have gotten the ribbon before I washed her."

Fortunately, his sister had left a ribbon hanging on her doorknob, so Dick was back down the stairs and out to the yard in seconds.

"Pansy, come back here!" he yelled as he saw her heading for the road. "Here, Pansy. Here's something for you!" He held out his hand, pretending to have a tidbit for the little pig.

Pansy looked back for only an instant, but it was long enough for Dick to catch up to her. In a flash he had her in his hands.

"Now you look here, Pansy!" he admonished. "You've got to change. Don't you want to be my pet? It's lots better than living out in the pigsty. You've got to stay clean from now on, do you hear? Clean, Pansy, clean!"

The little pig had had time to dirty only her feet, and a quick dip back in the tub took care of that. Dick rubbed the unwilling pet thoroughly, until her skin was a shiny, glowing pink. Then he tied the blue ribbon around her fat neck and made a big bow under her triple chin.

He picked her up under her two front legs, as if he were holding up a baby, and gazed approvingly at her loveliness. "Why, you're as good as a lamb," he tried to convince himself. Then he held her a little closer and sniffed hard. "Nope! You won't pass yet, I'm afraid. Let's see—some of Mom's perfume ought to help. Now Pansy, *please* stay here until I get it. *Please!*"

After another mad dash up and down the stairs, Dick was back with his mother's cologne bottle. Sure enough, Pansy was not where he had left her. She was rooting in Mother's flowers. He yanked her out and wiped her runny nose with a rag. Then he sprinkled her liberally with perfume.

"There!" He grinned with satisfaction. "That's how I'm going to keep you from now on. You're never going to get dirty again!"

He ran into the house. Mother and her guests were still talking, but soon Dick got Mother's attention. "Mother, may I please bring Pansy in? She's all scrubbed clean, and she even smells nice!"

Dick's pleading eyes must have touched Mother's heart, because she replied, "Well, if she's really as clean as all that, you can bring her in, but only for a few minutes."

Dick was out of the house so fast that Mother's words trailed away behind him. At last his pet could come into the house!

But when he reached the yard, there was no baby

pig to be seen! Quickly he looked in the flowers where Pansy had been rooting. Then he ran to the road and looked up and down. He simply couldn't bring himself to look in the most logical place to find a pig—the pigpen. But finally there was no other place to look. And, of course, there she was.

Her perfumed skin was plastered with foul-smelling, oozy mud. Her lovely blue ribbon was now a drippy string dangling between her front feet.

Dick couldn't hold back the tears. Why, oh why, couldn't that little pig stay clean and just be a nice pet?

That evening Dad put his arm around Dick and asked, "Why aren't you playing with Pansy?"

Then Dick told him the whole miserable tale. "What makes her like that?" he asked.

"Well, son, you did your best to clean her up. But she still has a piggy heart. She loves the mud and dirt, and as long as she's a pig inside, she'll never be anything but a pig, no matter how clean you make her on the outside."

Pansy grew fast and was soon too big to be an appealing pet. For several more years Dick carried in his heart a longing for a lamb.

Then, when he was 11, his dream came true! He got a real live lamb to love and care for. He made little Lucy a soft bed in a box near the kitchen stove and tenderly cared for her. She rewarded him with gentle nudges and nibbles of his fingers. When he brushed her white, curly wool and tied a ribbon around her neck, she made a charming picture. She looked as lovely in the evening as she had in the morning. She *stayed* clean. Now Dick better understood Dad's explanation of Pansy Pig's dirty ways.

Today Dick is a minister. Whenever he reads the words of Luke 11:39, 40—"You Pharisees clean the outside of the cup and dish, but inside you are full of greed and wickedness!"—he thinks of Pansy. And he's glad he chose to be one of Jesus' lambs.

8

Adventure in Lion Country

by Goldie M. Down

s it really lion country?" Bob's eyes were as round as saucers as he waited for his friend's reply.

"Sure is." Roger tossed a sleeping bag onto the roof rack of the old car. "We've been to the game sanctuary dozens of times, and we've always seen lions and elephants and plenty of other animals."

"I made a list last time we went camping there," his younger brother, Joey, added. "We saw giraffes and wildebeests and Thompson's gazelles and zebras and buffaloes and monkeys and warthogs and—"

"Boy, they're funny animals," Roger chuckled. "Warthogs look like pigs, only they have sharp, curved tusks and thin little tails as straight as a pencil."

"Except for the tuft of hair on the end," put in Joey.

"Yeah, and when they're alarmed, they race off

into the bush with their ridiculous, skinny tails sticking straight up into the air like ships' masts."

The boys laughed as they packed all the food and camping gear into the cars, but Bob's laughter was tinged with nervousness. His family had only recently come to Africa as missionaries, and he had never seen wild animals outside of a zoo. The flimsy tents that he was helping the boys stow into the car trunk did not seem like much protection from lion claws.

"Aren't you afraid of lions coming into the camp when you're asleep?" Bob tried to make his question sound casual.

"Not a bit. We built a big fire, or we keep a lantern burning all night. The big cats are afraid of fire and light, and they won't come near our camp."

"All aboard." Mr. Byron, the father of Roger and Joey, tucked in a bundle of last-minute items and slammed the trunk shut. "Is everyone ready to go?"

"Yes." Everyone in the four families nodded in unison as they climbed into their respective cars. Two more families were to join them at an appointed place, and everyone seemed excited at the prospect of a weekend of camping in the famous Serengeti Game Reserve in Tanzania, Africa.

The dusty miles ticked by, punctuated with delighted squeals as the children pointed out and identified various animals along the way.

"There's an ostrich on the left."

"Oh, I thought that was a bush. See his long neck?"

"Wait till you see a giraffe, Bob. They *really* have long necks."

"Is that a zebra hiding in the long grass over there?"

By evening they had reached the campsite and found the other two families waiting.

"We saw everything except lions today," Joey said disappointedly as he and Bob helped Roger pound in pegs and erect their tent. To their great joy, the three boys were being allowed to sleep in a tent all by themselves.

"Aw, it sometimes happens like that." Roger tied a tent rope with the air of an expert. "There might not be any around here, but we could see plenty tomorrow. One time we came across a pride under a big tree. They had eaten a whole wildebeest and were as full and lazy as anything."

"I'm glad there *aren't* any lions here," Bob muttered under his breath. He didn't mind the idea of seeing lions from the safety of a closed car, but this semicircle of small tents seemed but little shelter when wild beasts were roaming free.

After supper the group gathered around the campfire and sang until they were hoarse. Mr. Byron conducted evening worship, and soon the group began to scatter as the families straggled off to bed.

As self-appointed camp superintendent, Mr. Byron rolled more logs onto the fire and built up a bright blaze. He lit his porta-gas lamp and hung it high on the pole at the front of his tent. Its bright light could be seen from a great distance.

"That will discourage any predators that might be around," he explained as he lifted the flap and crawled into his own tent. Being the most experienced camper, he felt responsible for the rest of the group.

Soon the last murmur of voices died away, and silence enveloped the camp. But not everyone was asleep. In the boys' tent Roger tossed restlessly. The bright light from his father's lamp shone through the thin walls of the tent.

Bob was not asleep either. "What's the matter?" he asked as Roger squirmed around for the umpteenth time.

"I can't get to sleep with that light shining in my eyes," Roger grunted irritably. "I think I'll turn if off."

"Oh, you can't do that." Bob raised his head in alarm. "It has to be there to keep the wild beasts away. You told me that yourself."

"I said 'light *or* fire,'" Roger corrected grumpily. "There's a huge fire blazing out there. It will be hours before it dies down, and, anyway, I'm sure the men have arranged for someone to wake up and put more wood on it at intervals."

"But I'm sure we need the lamp, too," Bob protested. "Your father wouldn't want you to turn it off."

"Aw, don't be a scaredy-cat." Roger seemed even

more determined, and he crept out and turned off the lamp.

Once the bright light was gone, both boys fell asleep. And as they slept, the campfire crackled, and flames threw weird shadows on the circle of tents and cars. Hours passed. The last log was consumed, and the flames died to embers.

It was sometime between 2:00 and 3:00 in the morning when Mr. Byron was awakened by the jerking and swaying of his tent wall. Again and again the tent jerked as if someone were pulling on the ropes.

"It must be Pastor Peters playing a joke on me," Mr. Byron chuckled to himself. "If he thinks that he can scare me that way—"

At that moment something heavy thudded onto the tent roof, and the canvas was pushed down hard on Mr. Byron's shoulder, pinning him to the ground. He heard a scraping, scratching sound. Instantly his drowsy mind alerted to danger.

"Lions!" he shouted at the top of his voice as he struggled to free himself. "Lions in the camp!"

Mrs. Byron reached for the flashlight that she had left beside her pillow. All the others in the camp awoke, and shouts of alarm came from all directions.

"Where are the matches?" The noise had caused the lion to back off the tent, and Mr. Byron was able to crawl out of his sleeping bag. "Give me the matches, and I'll light the lamp. I can't understand what made it go out. There was plenty of gas."

Trembling with excitement, he lifted the tent flap, and Mrs. Byron kept the flashlight directed outside. Three pairs of glowing eyes reflected the beam of light.

"Keep it shining on them," Mr. Byron encouraged as he reached up and unhooked the lantern. "They won't come any nearer if that light is in their eyes."

By now the whole camp was astir. Flashlight beams roved in all directions, picking out glowing eyes backed by dark, heavy forms. Two of the men dashed to their cars and frantically pressed their horn buttons.

The noise of horns and the shouts and excited voices, all combined with the lantern and flashlights, finally got the message across to the lions that they were not welcomed visitors. One by one the gleaming eyes disappeared as the animals slunk back into the shadows and were lost in the darkness.

As soon as they felt it was safe to do so, the campers gathered around the newly blazing fire. All talked at once, giving their versions of the lions' visit. Then above the hubbub Mr. Byron's voice was heard clearly.

"Friends, if it had not been for the ever-present watchfulness of the angels, this incident could have had serious consequences. The fire had died down, and the lantern was out. What I want to know is how it got *turned* out."

Dead silence greeted his question. For a long moment nothing was heard except the crackling of the fire and the soft hiss of the lamp. Roger swallowed hard and avoided Bob's eyes. Too late he regretted his showing off. He had known very well that light was necessary for the protection of the campers, but he had honestly thought that there were no lions around and that the firelight would be sufficient.

Again he swallowed hard. The words seemed to stick in his throat, half strangling him. "I did it, Dad."

"You?" Mr. Byron stared in surprise at his son. "You knew better than anyone else here how much we needed that light. I'll deal with you later, but I do appreciate your telling the truth."

Turning his attention back to the group, Mr. Byron said, "Friends, the lions will not return tonight. Before we go back to bed, let us thank God for protecting us from the results of my son's foolish action."

9

Quicksand

by Margery Wilson

Howdy, neighbor."

John and his father looked up to see a man on horseback riding into the barnyard.

"My name's Jeremy, Jake Jeremy. Live down the road toward Myers about six miles."

"Nice of you to stop by. I'm Harold Jones, and this is my son, John."

The two farmers leaned against the weathered barn, discussing crops, cattle, and weather. John loved these rest times and soaked up the conversation.

"Say, did anyone tell you about the quicksand down on the river backwater?" Jake asked.

"Quicksand? Why, I've got cattle down there."

"Oh, stock usually avoid it. Seem to sense the danger, unless they get chased into it or something freakish happens. I know an animal or two starved in that quicksand before anyone found them."

"Here, I'll saddle horses for John and me. Let's take a look."

As the three rode, John listened to the men discussing the horrors of quicksand. Jake pointed out different patches of it along the riverbank pasture, which turned into an island when the Yellowstone River overflowed its banks in flood season.

"I tell you, Mr. Jones, quicksand is deadly stuff. Some of it has a bottom, and some of it just swallows everything that sets foot in it—man, animal, trucks, or trains. Works slow but sure."

"And I've heard that the more you try to get out, the more it seems to pull you down," Father added. "Be best just to lie down and hope the good Lord will send someone to rescue you."

"Yep. That's best. Spreads your weight over a larger area. But a cow can't spread herself out. She just sinks out of sight and starves on the way."

"I can never thank you enough for taking time to show us these danger spots. We'll keep checking them and hope for the best."

With that, John and his father rode back toward the big old farmhouse.

Quicksand filled John's thoughts that evening. "Dad, do you really believe what Jake Jeremy told you today about quicksand being deadly stuff?"

"Sure do. I've never met up with quicksand, but

you hear terrible tales about it."

"But Dad, that sand was pretty firm. It didn't look like anything would sink in it. Oh, it did look a little different, but not dangerous."

"You can't go by looks."

"Oh, he's just scaring you. Maybe he wants you to move so he can rent this place."

"That's your imagination, but danger is real. In fact, I want you to check those spots every other day at least. I'd hate to lose an animal."

"Well, I'm not scared!" John declared.

"I hope you don't have to learn the hard way. After the spring flood next year, that quicksand area will be soupy. We'll heave some big rocks into it, and you can watch them disappear. That might scare you."

John forgot quicksand during the winter at school. The Yellowstone River usually ran wide and deep, but come late May and June it spread itself into the lowlands, creating ponds and islands.

One day John rode through the acres of pasture on his saddle horse, counting stock for his father. The big river served as a natural fence along the river pasture, since none of the horses or cows tried to cross it there.

Suddenly John heard a strange sound. He galloped upriver toward the sound and found a young colt nervously prancing around. "Say, that's Queenie's colt," he said to himself.

An anguished nicker beyond the bushes split the air.

John sped right to the sound and found Queenie helpless, with quicksand well up her sides. He stared in unbelief at the sight of the big saddle horse imprisoned in a sea of mud.

When the mare saw John, she lifted her weary head to nicker again, pouring all the desperation of her soul into a plea for help.

John saw the sad situation before him and remembered his arrogant skepticism about quicksand. He also remembered that his father had told him to check the quicksand spots every other day. Why hadn't he come here yesterday?

"OK, Queenie, I'll get help. Easy now," John soothed. "You're out there more than a hundred feet. I can't get to you now. Easy!"

John rode like fury to search for his father and tell him about the horse in the quicksand. The two quickly hitched a team to the wagon, throwing in boards, another doubletree, hammers, nails, rope, hay, oats, and everything else they thought they might need.

Both of them called assurance to the mare when they rumbled up to the bank and surveyed the nearly impossible task before them.

"She's facing us. Must have suddenly realized what she was in and had enough speed to turn around and head back," Father observed.

"Or maybe she just wandered into it coming up from the water hole, and something frightened her into making a run for the bank here. Dad, she can't even struggle anymore."

"Poor thing has worn herself out. Probably been here a couple of days. Here, take these boards and make a walkway out to her. You're a lot lighter than I am. Keep throwing a board ahead of you and walking on it to throw the next one down."

John plopped boards onto the soupy sand while his father took smaller boards and nailed together a platform about three feet wide and six feet long. He worked fast, squinting every so often at the nearly submerged animal to spur himself to greater speed.

"Now, John, tie that light rope around your waist and carry this little platform out there. You'll have to walk quickly. Don't stop if you can help it."

John ran along his boardwalk and tossed the platform next to the mare, returning for a shovel and a heavy, one-inch rope. "Want this rope around her neck?"

"Not at first. It would probably break her neck if we pulled her out that way."

"You don't expect me to get this rope behind her front legs!"

"I expect you to try. Dig a trench in front of her." For a moment Mr. Jones leaned against the wagon in near despair. "I have to drive the team. They're used to me and will work better for me."

John sprawled out flat on the platform and dug down, down in the sandy ooze. Taking the end of the rope that he had draped over the mare's head for safe-keeping, he shoved it through the soupy mud behind her front legs.

"Straddle her back now and see whether you can get your work platform over to her other side," yelled his father from the bank.

John dug from the other side and reached his hand into the mud, fishing for the end of the rope he had shoved into it. "Got it!"

"Good. Tie a knot up on top—a bowline, not a slip knot."

John wondered how he could ever hang on to that muddy, slippery rope to tie any knot at all.

"Now around her neck. And dig a trench around her if you can."

"A trench all the way around? Why?"

"Maybe we can get some of that water that's not too far behind her to wash in around her."

"Won't that make her sink farther, Dad?"

"I don't think so. I hope it will break the suction effect of that quicksand."

While John struggled with the rope and dug the trench about the mare, a hungry little colt ran back and forth on the bank. The half-starved baby tried to nurse from the wagon team, but the workhorses kicked him away. The colt made Father's work extra difficult as he unhitched the team from the wagon.

"Looks like we're ready for the long haul, son." The older man tied the heavy rope securely to the doubletree behind the horses.

He stood beside the team and talked gently, telling them that this would be a hard pull. Suddenly, a splintering sound broke the tension. John groaned when he saw the doubletree hanging in two pieces.

"Some luck." Father's voice sounded like a sob. "Good thing we brought an extra doubletree, but it will take me a while to get it on."

"I hate to tell you, but we haven't even budged her yet, Dad."

John patted the mare, giving her more assurance than he really felt himself. The old hardwood doubletree had served to pull some big loads, so maybe the next one wouldn't hold, either. Maybe they wouldn't be able to pull her out.

"Ready again," yelled Mr. Jones.

John could hear him urging the team to do their utmost. Twice now their pulling power had failed to move her. He sagged against the mare's back, thinking of the animal's fate if they failed.

Once more the workhorses leaned into their collars for a mighty pull, as if they realized what they had to do.

John felt the submerged mare surge forward a few inches, a bit more, and then with a final burst of strength the team on the bank pulled the mare free of her murky prison.

"Will she ever be strong enough to get up?" shouted John as he ran back across the boards.

Father forgot about his own weight and ran the length of the boardwalk to fill his old felt hat with the muddy water in the trench. Then he rushed back to the pitiful horse. The mare quickly sucked the hat dry.

Then John grabbed the hat and ran for more water. He washed the mud from her udder so the hungry colt could suck.

Realizing that the terrible ordeal was over, Queenie made a supreme effort and staggered to an uncertain, wobbly stand.

"We nearly lost this horse," said Mr. Jones as John brought the hay and oats to Queenie.

"I know, Dad, and it would have been my fault. I haven't been paying much attention to those quick-sand spots that you told me to check." John steeled himself, knowing that his father could be pretty stern when someone neglected their duties.

"Well, I know you never would have forgiven yourself if we'd failed to get her out. We can thank God and a good team for that. Quicksand is like sin—the farther away from it the better."

10

The Snake and I

by Elfa Childers

The sun scorched the top of my head. The hot earth blistered my bare feet. I felt as though I were in the middle of a huge frying pan, waiting for a giant spatula to turn me over. Wiping my forehead with the back of my hand, I decided to leave the weeding until the sun was less intense and walk to my father's science lab to see if anything new was developing.

I glanced down at my feet and contemplated whether or not I should put some shoes on. Mother was always warning me of the dangers surrounding our mission in Rhodesia, Africa, with all its snakes, scorpions, and other menaces, but I found her reminders an unwanted irritation, so I decided to forgo the shoes and socks.

The minute I opened the door to the lab I could sense the suppressed excitement. My eyes scanned the objects in the room and rested on a wooden box in the center of one of the lab tables. Out of this box issued a slow, hideous breathing sound, which permeated the whole room. It sounded to me like a man afflicted with emphysema who was snoring.

There were several people in the room, and I made my way over to where my father was talking to Mr. Tarr, the business manager of the mission. My intention was to discover what was in the box by eavesdropping a little.

"You know, Bob," Mr. Tarr was saying, "this snake is strong and vicious. He's trapped, and he knows it. If we slip up and he escapes, we'll have trouble on our hands for sure."

"Yes, I'm well aware of that," Father agreed. "But if we plan everything just right, we should be able to move him into this new cage safely. He's a fine specimen and would be a great asset to my snake collection."

A snake! I moved closer to the box and tried to see through the little slits, but it was too dark inside. Father had several kinds of snakes in the lab, but I could tell that this one was different from the others.

Once Father had caught a poisonous puff adder in our neighbor's kitchen. From appearances the puff adder seemed slow and lazy, but when it struck at a victim, its backward aim was tremendously quick and sure.

Father had two black mambas that he had caught

outside his office. They too looked insignificant, but are believed to be the deadliest snakes in the world.

The door to the lab opened and heralded the entrance of my mother and Mr. Tarr's son, Alan.

"Hi," I greeted Alan when he came closer to me. "What are you doing here?"

"Good morning," he responded, frowning a little at my query. "Your father caught a banded cobra in the mechanics shop this morning. They've been working all day to build him a decent cage and to organize everything to keep the snake here in the lab. Right now I'm here for the same reason you are."

I started to give my opinion of this remark, but my attention was diverted to what my mother was saying. "Bob, what's this about another snake? You know this is dangerous business, and I think you should forget the whole scheme and get rid of the horrid thing before somebody is killed."

Excitement claimed me as I turned my attention once more to Alan.

"OK, Alan," I said. "What do you know about the snake?"

"What would you like to know?" This was accompanied by a noticeable increase in his chest measurement.

"How long would it take for a person to die if they were bitten?" I asked.

Alan arched his brows and prepared to send forth

a stream of intelligence in my direction. He considered this a perfect opportunity to exaggerate the importance of his two-year advantage over my 14 years.

"Well, Elfa," he answered pompously, "let me see. If the cobra were to inject five drops of poison into a normal-sized adult, the venom would attack the nerve impulses and interfere with the diaphragm and the heartbeat in less than five minutes."

I'd heard all I wanted to hear, so I let him ramble on while I turned my attention to the more immediate matters at hand. My father had apparently made most of the arrangements for the exchange of the snake and was explaining the procedure to Mother. I was amazed at how long it had taken them to figure out exactly what had to be done, and who they wanted to do it.

I decided that I wanted a part to perform also, so I went and stood close to Father, nodding at my mother at appropriate intervals. By looking involved, I tried to convince everyone who bothered to notice that I had been instrumental in making all the plans, and that I intended to help execute them.

"You're not seriously considering letting Elfa help, are you?" my mother exclaimed.

I held my breath while my father glanced down at me. I looked up at him and pleaded silently, muscles visibly tensed.

"Sure I am," he added. "She's going to stand behind the new cage and hold this heavy cardboard strip over the hole in the side when I slide up the front."

I grinned, grabbed the cardboard, and disappeared around the lab table. Mother and Father conferred back and forth until he had convinced her to stay and take part by covering the opposite hole in the cage with some wooden planking.

I sauntered over to Alan and said airily, "Well, Alan, you'd better leave now. We have to get to business with the snake, and there really isn't any room for onlookers." I exaggerated the last word and then lowered my nose a little to see his reaction.

"Oh, I'm going to help too." His tone implied that his job was of key importance and that he would perform it with complete devotion. "I have to hold up the sliding glass front," he proudly announced.

I wasn't too pleased with this turn of events, but my retort was postponed by Father's interruption.

"Everyone take your places, and we'll get started," Father ordered. "We're ready to go."

With that, he picked up the snake box and brought it over to the front of the new cage on the floor. When the box was moved, the menacing sound inside grew more intense. "Sounds hideous, doesn't he?" Father commented.

"It's no wonder that the snake is used as a symbol for sin," Mr. Tarr replied. "Not only did Satan use a snake in the Garden of Eden, but each one seems to portray the same characteristics as sin."

"Yes, they are fascinating creatures, aren't they?" Alan had to put in his two cents' worth.

"I find any kind of snake to he utterly repulsive, yet irresistible at the same time," Mr. Tarr continued.

"I've never had any trouble resisting them," Mother said. "Come on, let's get this over with."

Father slowly raised the glass front and then glanced around to be sure that all was in order. "If this snake gets loose, he will be just as dangerous as sin out of control, that I can tell you," he said.

"If that happens, I'm heading for the back of the room, so don't anyone else go there. That's mine!" I said to no one in particular.

"The light fixtures on the ceiling would be too low for me if this monster escapes," Alan stated.

I darted a baleful glance in his direction, but Mother forestalled any further comment by telling us both to be quiet and pay attention. All the while, Father was drilling a hole in the back of the box and putting some wire through the hole to push the snake out from the dark box into the lighter and bigger cage. Every time the snake came out, he'd see all of us through the glass top and go back into the box. Each time I saw him, I felt myself go clammier and shakier. He looked so big and vicious.

Alan gave a shudder at my side, and the glass front slipped a little in his hands. Father gave a warning glance, and the glass was immediately pulled back into position. I could hear the snake's body rasp along the bottom of the box. My hand began to sweat against the heavy cardboard, and I could feel my hair plastered against the wetness of my forehead.

Father muttered something under his breath, gave a huge shove, and succeeded in pushing the snake from the box into the cage. With horror I saw that the length of the snake exceeded seven feet, and he was about four inches in diameter. Upon entering his new domain, he immediately traversed each corner for a way of escape. With lightning speed he sent his powerful and ugly nose along every crevice, and met with total resistance until he came to my piece of cardboard.

By this time my whole body was a mass of shaking nerves, and when I felt the pressure against my hand, I was convinced that my time had come. Feeling the slight give from the cardboard, the snake pushed with tremendous strength, and the cardboard bent into my palm. Hypnotized, I watched as the snake pushed aside the cardboard and slid his head between my extended fingers. A shock seemed to run through my left arm when I felt my fingers pushed apart by that big, smooth head.

Then I gave a yell and jumped back from the cage. Mother jumped onto one of the lab tables, Alan gave a leap for the lights, and I flew to the back of the room. Everyone was yelling, screaming, or crying. The snake curled itself on the floor and reared its upper body while flattening its hood.

It took 30 minutes and some hasty reorganizing, but the snake was finally recaptured and safely locked in his cage.

Then, after we thanked God that no one was hurt, I went home to put on my shoes and socks. Any temptation to leave my feet bare would henceforth go unheeded. So would any temptation to act self-important!

11

Trumpet Remembers

by Juliana Lewis

Watch it, Jeff!" A man's voice rang out like a shot across the wet passenger deck.

Jeff Johnson withdrew his gangling form from the guardrail and laughed. "Don't worry, Dad. I'm not going to topple overboard! I want to see Trumpet too much to fall in now!"

Then a pensive look settled over his face as he repeated to Dad the same question he'd asked himself a dozen times during their long voyage from America to India: "Do you think Trumpet will still remember me?"

"I wouldn't count on it, son. After all, six years is a long time—long enough for even an elephant to forget."

Yes, Jeff admitted to himself, *six years is a long time.* Six years ago he was celebrating his seventh birthday at Rayo's bamboo home. Rayo, son of the caretaker of the elephant compound, had been very close to Jeff in those days. If it had not been for him, Jeff might never have met Trumpet.

At last Jeff and his father found themselves once again on the teeming shores of India. Jeff had almost forgotten just how busy the city streets could be, filled with dogs, oxcarts, horse cabs, and vendors. But all were avoided by the skilled taxi driver, who soon deposited them at their hotel.

"Wait here in the room, Jeff," Dr. Johnson said after they had carried their luggage upstairs. "I want to go phone Dr. Martin long-distance and let him know when to expect us."

Dr. Martin had been sent to India to work at a village hospital, just as Jeff's father had in the past, and in the same small village—that of Rayo's people. Since Jeff's mother had died when he was born, he and his father had lived in the home of Rayo's parents, where they had become accepted as family members. Now the U.S. government had sent Dr. Johnson back to India, but only for a short inspection tour.

While his father was gone, Jeff gazed out at the harbor, where the great sea seemed to be a continuation of the gentle ripples of the sun-warmed sand. He had missed India, the rugged Himalaya Mountains, the wide Ganges River, and the marble temples so beautiful by moonlight. But most of all he had missed Trumpet.

His mind drifted back to that day when Rayo had first taken him to the elephant compound. "Look, Rayo. I like *him* most." Jeff had singled out the smallest of the lot—a youngster tugging mightily at the branches of a mango tree.

"Ah, that is Trumpet," Rayo had replied. "He is a rare one, born in captivity three years ago. He is smart but has the call of the wild in him."

From that first moment Jeff felt affection for Trumpet, with his unusual rough white skin and pert, pointed lower lip. And the friendship wasn't all one-sided, for Trumpet soon showed an equal devotion to Jeff.

Within a week Jeff could call, "Come, Trumpet—time for your bath," and Trumpet would rush with delight toward the shallow river where Jeff waited to scrub him. More than once during the proceedings Jeff would be surprised by well-aimed sprays from the trunk of his playful pal.

For two years they had spent a part of each day together. Jeff fed Trumpet carrots and rubbed the tiny bristles on his head. Trumpet enfolded Jeff in his trunk, lifting him up for topside rides. Neither seemed to need more than the other for companionship. Only on occasion, when the distant thundering of wild jungle elephants came to their ears, did Jeff sense moments of restlessness in his friend. Trumpet would pause, cocking his head as if listening to a faraway summons.

Once during the monsoon season when Trumpet remained too long in the dampness and developed pneumonia, Jeff faithfully nursed him through the illness until he was well again. That was just before Dr. Johnson had been transferred back to the States, and though Jeff hadn't seen Trumpet since then, he hadn't forgotten their friendship.

"Son," the sound of his father's voice brought Jeff back to the present, "we'd better turn in now. Dr. Martin and Rayo are expecting us tomorrow, and we should get an early start."

A colorful sunrise awakened Jeff, and it wasn't long before he and his father were seated comfortably in a cross-country train. By evening they arrived at the village station, where Dr. Martin and Rayo and his family were waiting. Rayo had changed a lot, but Jeff was quick to recognize him. So the two began to recount old times.

Jeff could hardly wait to ask about Trumpet. "How is he? Where is he? When can I see him?"

With downcast eyes Rayo explained, "After you left, Trumpet became sad and refused to eat. Not even the choicest bits tempted him. Then one morning as I was taking him for a bath, we heard wild elephants stampeding in the distance. Before I could stop him, Trumpet raised his trunk and charged off through the jungle. I have never seen him since, but I often hear of him. He has the reputation of being a leader and protector of the herd."

Jeff tried to hide his disappointment at not being able to greet his old friend. He had even hoped that his father might permit him to take Trumpet back to America.

"How is your parrot?" he asked Rayo, to change the subject.

"Fine," Rayo answered. "I have another pet to show you, too—a monkey I think you will like."

Jeff enjoyed playing with the monkey and the parrot, getting reacquainted with the elephant compound, and swimming with Rayo. He watched new elephants being tamed, but all the while, thoughts of Trumpet remained in the back of his mind.

The day before leaving, Jeff wandered into the jungle. Walking farther than he'd intended, he sat down to rest by a large tree root before starting back. The warmth of the sun relaxed him so completely that before long he fell asleep.

The coolness of late day finally aroused Jeff. Opening his eyes, he shut them again quickly in fright. Coiled near his feet, with eyes trained on him, lay one of the most dreaded of snakes, a cobra. Jeff remained absolutely still, a cold perspiration breaking out on his forehead. Dusk descended, but neither he nor the cobra altered positions.

Suddenly the silence was broken by a tremendous noise. Breaking their way through the underbrush came an elephant herd in a single file. At the head walked a proud white beauty.

"Trumpet!" called Jeff.

Trumpet stopped still and raised his powerful trunk. Then he surged forward, bringing his foot down with one heavy, crushing blow on the hooded head of the cobra.

Jeff was at Trumpet's side in no time, crying with relief and happiness. He fondly rubbed the tough wrinkles of Trumpet's hide and the battle scar on his neck. Trumpet encircled Jeff with his long trunk, lifted him to his back, and unhesitatingly headed toward the compound, careful to guard his rider against the sting of obstructing twigs and branches. At the edge of the jungle Trumpet stopped, and Jeff understood.

He understood that Trumpet was leaving him here so that each of them would be free—free to remember and free to follow his own call toward the hills of home.

12

A Joyful Noise

by Mary H. Duplex

Joanne ran straight from school to Mrs. Penworthy's house and quietly let herself in. *I shouldn't have stayed to help Mrs. Sperry,* she thought. *I almost forgot it's Tuesday.* She glanced at the grandfather clock beside the stairway and sighed with relief. She wasn't late for her piano lesson after all.

She sat down in the big wooden chair outside the studio door to wait. The house was quiet except for the tick of the clock. Maybe Mike had already finished his lesson.

Joanne opened the studio door and peeked inside. The drapes were drawn, and no one was at the piano. She smiled. Now she could pet Major while she waited for Mrs. Penworthy. The old black-and-white border collie was 16, stiff in the joints, and almost blind. But he always wagged his tail whenever she came near.

Joanne moved past the shiny black grand piano in the middle of the room to Major's bed in the corner. It was empty. *Mrs. Penworthy must have taken him for a walk,* she thought. She sat down at the piano and picked out a tune while she waited.

When Mrs. Penworthy finally appeared in the doorway, Joanne smiled and got up from the piano bench. "Did you and Major have a nice walk?" she asked.

Mrs. Penworthy clamped her hand over her mouth to stifle a soft moan and dabbed at her red, puffy eyes with a handkerchief. "Major died in his sleep last night," she said at last.

"Oh, I'm so sorry," Joanne sympathized. "He was such a nice dog."

"He was all I had." Mrs. Penworthy's voice was choked with tears. "There will be no lessons today. Please go now." She turned and hurried out of the room.

Joanne let herself out quietly and started home.

"Have you finished your lesson already?" Kelly asked when she met Joanne coming down the street. "I'd better hurry, or I'll be late for mine."

"Mrs. Penworthy isn't giving lessons today." Joanne explained about the dog.

"That's too bad," Kelly said, falling into step beside her. "I liked Major too."

In the weeks that followed, Joanne tried to cheer

her music teacher up. But each time Mrs. Penworthy looked at Major's empty bed, her eyes filled with tears. Joanne wished there was something she could do to help her feel better.

On her way home from her lesson one afternoon Joanne saw Kelly roller-skating toward the park. "You're going to be late for your lesson," she called. "You'd better hurry."

"I'm not taking lessons from Mrs. Penworthy anymore," Kelly said. "It's no fun going there since Major died. Mrs. Penworthy always looks so sad, and she never laughs or plays neat little tunes on the piano the way she used to. I'm going to start taking lessons from that new teacher over on Third Street. Mike started there yesterday, and he says she's lots of fun. Why don't you change too?"

Joanne shook her head. "I've always taken lessons from Mrs. Penworthy. She's a good teacher, and I like her even if she is unhappy over Major's death."

Kelly shrugged. "You can stay with her if you want to, but I don't like being around sad people." She skated away.

Kelly's right, Joanne thought. *I always feel sad after my lessons too. If something doesn't happen soon to cheer up Mrs. Penworthy, she'll lose the rest of her students.*

By the time she reached home, Joanne decided on a plan. When Joey's dog had been killed by a car, his parents had bought him a new puppy. It hadn't taken Joey long to learn to love it, too. But she would have to find a special dog to take Major's place. Mrs. Penworthy had had him since he was 2 months old.

After school the next day, Joanne took all the money out of her desk bank and went to the local animal shelter. "I would like to see the puppies, please," she said.

"We don't have any pups right now," the attendant said, "but I can show you the big dogs."

Joanne followed him from cage to cage. There were all kinds of dogs, but Joanne didn't think any of them were right for Mrs. Penworthy.

The next morning she asked all of her friends at school if they knew anyone who had puppies for sale.

"We have some boxer puppies. They'll be ready next month," one boy offered.

"Thanks, but I don't think a boxer would do," Joanne said, wondering where to look next. On the way home from school she stopped at the pet shop. The only puppies they had were toy poodles, and they cost more than she could afford.

For the next month Joanne continued to search. She checked the pet column in the newspaper every day and went back each week to the animal shelter and the pet shop. But she couldn't find the special puppy she was looking for.

Maybe this isn't such a good idea after all, she said to

herself. *I'll have to think of some other way to help Mrs. Penworthy.*

One day Joanne's mother was waiting when she came home from school. "I'm going out to Mr. Frazer's farm to buy some eggs. Would you like to come along?"

"I guess so," Joanne answered.

Mr. Frazer came out to meet them when Mother parked the car in his front yard. "I hope I have enough eggs," he said. "I took a shipment of eggs into the city yesterday afternoon, and I had a bit of trouble this morning."

Joanne and her mother followed him toward the egg room at the far end of the chicken house, where the eggs were cleaned and sorted for size. As they passed the tool shed Joanne heard a whimper. "I think your dog got closed up in the shed," she said. "Would you like me to let him out?"

Mr. Frazer frowned. "Not my dog. It's a pup somebody dropped off in the middle of the night. I heard the car slow down, and early this morning I found him barking at the chickens. This is the best laying flock I've ever had, but he scared them so badly that I've gotten less than a dozen eggs from them today. Guess some folks don't realize that a chicken farm is no place for a pup."

"May I see him?" Joanne asked.

"Don't let him out," Mr. Frazer warned. He opened the door wide enough for Joanne to slip through and then closed it behind her.

The small dusty window didn't let in much light. When Joanne's eyes adjusted to the dimness, she looked around. The puppy was huddled in a corner. He was thin and dirty and his hair was matted, but Joanne knew the minute she saw him that he was special. He was marked exactly like Major.

She crouched down to pet him. With a whimper of joy the puppy bounded into her arms and licked her face with a quick pink tongue. Joanne giggled and held him close. "I've been looking and looking for you," she said.

Joanne opened the door a little way. "Please, may I have him, Mr. Frazer?"

"If your mother agrees," Mr. Frazer answered. Mother looked at the puppy and nodded.

Joanne held the squirming puppy on her lap all the way home. "I'm going to give him a bath first thing," she decided.

Mother wrinkled up her nose and smiled. "He can certainly use one. And you'll have to fix a bed for him in the garage tonight."

"Oh, I'm not going to keep him," Joanne explained. "I'm going to give him to Mrs. Penworthy."

Her mother frowned thoughtfully. "I'm not sure that's such a good idea, Joanne. Mr. Brewster offered her a dog, and she wouldn't even look at it."

"But this puppy is special," Joanne said. "I know

Mrs. Penworthy will love him."

"You can try, of course, but don't be too disappointed if she refuses to take him."

When the puppy was bathed and dried, his soft black-and-white coat shone, and there was mischief in his dark eyes. "Oh, you're so cute; I'd love to keep you myself," Joanne said. "But I know someone who needs you more."

She put on her jacket and tucked the puppy inside. "I'll be back in a few minutes," she called and hurried down the street.

Joanne slipped quietly into Mrs. Penworthy's studio. She placed the puppy in Major's bed. "Now you stay there and be quiet," she whispered. Then she turned and tiptoed toward the door. The puppy whined, then barked when he heard footsteps coming down the hall.

If Mrs. Penworthy sees me, she might not even look at the puppy, Joanne thought. She ducked quickly behind the drapes.

Mrs. Penworthy rushed into the room and stopped short. She glanced at Major's bed. "Oh, no!" she gasped and turned away. The puppy cried again. Mrs. Penworthy paused in the doorway.

Joanne held her breath. *Oh, please, please look at him,* she said silently.

Mrs. Penworthy stood there for a long moment, then slowly looked back. The puppy tilted his head to one side and whimpered. Mrs. Penworthy crossed the room to Major's bed. The puppy trembled with excitement and barked.

"You poor little thing; you look half starved." Mrs. Penworthy bent down and picked him up. "I don't know where you came from, but I suppose it wouldn't hurt to feed you just this once." She carried the squirming puppy down the hall toward the kitchen.

Joanne smiled as she closed the door softly and hurried home.

On Tuesday afternoon Joanne headed toward Mrs. Penworthy's for her lesson. *What if she didn't like the puppy after all?* she wondered. *I hope she didn't give it away.*

As Joanne started up the walk, she heard Mrs. Penworthy singing and playing a little tune on the piano. She was being accompanied by excited, high-pitched barks. Joanne opened the studio door. The puppy raced across the room to her, wagging his tail.

Mrs. Penworthy glanced up and smiled at Joanne. "Come in and meet my newest pupil," she said.

Joanne giggled. "Are you teaching him to sing?" she asked, petting the puppy.

Mrs. Penworthy laughed. "Hardly that," she answered. "Young Major and I were making a joyful noise unto the Lord."

Joanne grinned and said a grateful prayer of thanks. Mrs. Penworthy's laugh was the most joyful noise she'd heard in that room for a long time.

13

Spots

by Earl Bucknum

Spots had wandered into the fire station six years before as a stray puppy and had been quickly adopted by the firefighters. They taught him to roll over, sit up, play dead, and fetch any article on command. One of the firefighters said that Spots could do everything but slide down the fire pole, and if given the proper instruction, he could probably accomplish this trick.

The dog slept in a basket in the firefighters' sleeping quarters. When the big bell would sound the alarm in the middle of the night, he would leap out of his basket, barking loudly, and dash from bed to bed making sure all the firefighters were up and dressing.

If someone was slow in getting up, Spots would bark in their ear, leap onto the bed, take the covers in his mouth, and jerk them off. As the last firefighter slid down the pole, Spots, who seemed to be counting them, would dash down the stairs and onto the driver's seat of the leading engine.

On the way to the fire Spots would sit like a king on his throne, viewing the entire scene as the fire truck thundered through the busy traffic with its siren shrieking a warning to motorists to get out of the way. Sometimes Spots, not satisfied with the way the traffic was moving, would start barking continually, as if his contribution to the siren would miraculously part the sea of cars ahead.

Once the firefighters reached the scene of the fire, the dog would remain on his lofty perch, out of the way of the scurrying firefighters as they performed their hazardous duties. He would sometimes sit for hours until the fire was out or under control. Then he'd bark happily as the firefighters returned to their trucks for the homeward journey.

Late one night the fire bell clanged out its alarm. Spots dashed around barking wildly as the firefighters quickly leaped on the trucks and headed for a five-story apartment building almost four miles away. Traffic was light, so they reached the scene in a matter of minutes. Unfortunately, the fire had gotten a good start before the alarm went off. The entire building was a raging inferno with giant flames and black billowing smoke pouring out of the windows and doors.

Spots heard two firefighters talking. "I guess everyone is out," one firefighter shouted. "Too bad it had too much of a start for us to save the building."

"Yeah, the chief made a quick check," his buddy replied. "All the tenants seem to be out of the building."

The firefighters continued to pour water on the condemned structure in an effort to keep the fire from spreading.

Suddenly a large black cat dashed out through the smoke pouring from a doorway. He ran from one fire-fighter to another, as if requesting help. But all the firefighters were too busy with their hazardous duties to notice the animal.

Then the cat looked toward the fire truck where Spots was sitting on his lofty perch. Bounding swiftly up to the truck, it looked up and gave a pitiful meow. Now, Spots had chased many a cat away from the vicinity of the fire station. But this cat's manner was different somehow. It started toward the burning building, then returned to look up at Spots with another meow. Once more it started toward the fire and quickly returned. Suddenly Spots got the message. This big black cat wanted him to follow!

Spots hesitated because he had been taught to remain on the truck. But this time instinct seemed to be giving him an urgent message. Leaping off the truck, Spots pursued the cat, which looked back several times to make sure the dog was following.

The cat headed directly for a doorway at the end of the building and entered a smoke-filled hallway. About 50 feet down the hallway it stopped beside a man who was lying on the floor at the foot of a flight of stairs. As the two animals reached him, he opened his eyes and groaned, "It's you, Blackie. I knew you would bring help. My leg! Oh, my leg!" He gave another groan. "I see that you've tried to bring help, but what can this dog do?"

As if answering the man's question, Spots whirled around and raced for the outside door. Blackie seemed satisfied with Spots' actions and curled up next to the man.

When Spots reached the outside, he dashed up to two firefighters, seized one by the pant leg, and began tugging. Surprised to see him off the truck, one started to scold him. The dog dashed a short distance toward the burning building, then ran to the firefighter, barking excitedly all the time.

"I think he wants us to follow him," declared the second firefighter.

The two men stepped inside the doorway and felt their way down the smoky hallway. They found the man, with his cat still by his side, and quickly dragged him down the hallway and out into the open air. The two animals scrambled ahead of the firefighters, seeming to sense that the man was now in good hands.

Seconds after they reached the outside, a whole section of the building, including the doorway they had just passed through, collapsed with a fiery crash.

Looking back, one of the firefighters remarked, "That was too close. One more minute, and this fellow would have been a goner."

The emergency crew quickly administered oxygen, and the man opened his eyes. His first concern was for the two heroic animals that had saved his life. When assured that both animals were safe, he smiled and said, "God sent those two animals to save me."

Spots, the stray dalmatian, rode in the seat of honor all the way back to the firehouse.

14

God's Little Barbados

by Bonnie Wadewitz

Aunt Martha really didn't need another pet. She was already busy caring for three mangy dogs, a dozen assorted cats, a swaybacked duck with a misshapen bill, and five disheveled old roosters. But when she heard that Floyd Venner, her neighbor up the road, had given up hope for a tiny Barbados lamb, she begged to adopt the weak little orphan. That was her first mistake.

The tiny lamb, which she named Barbados, didn't stay tiny very long and soon became so mischievous that he exhausted even her vast store of patience. He butted her dogs, chewed on the cats' tails, and ate the corn intended for the roosters. He opened the screen door, sought out her bedroom, and claimed her best pillow for his personal resting place. When, in desperation, she tied him to a tree with a little rope, he immediately chewed it in two and continued his naughty behavior.

She asked Floyd Venner if he wanted his lamb back, but he didn't. That's when she offered him to us. "Please take him," she begged my father. "He'd make a fine pet for the children."

My sisters and I had a great time with him. When we got tired of his antics, we simply put him in the pasture with our flock. We did enjoy him immensely, but Father enjoyed him the most. He gave him a sugar lump every day and always had a pat on the head for him. He taught him to come when he called, "Little Barbados, Little Barbados!"

The frisky little fellow soon considered himself a member of the family and demanded all the privileges that went with it. He broke a hole through the screen door so he could be with us when we were having dinner. He learned to go upstairs to my room. One time he leaped onto the house roof from a picnic table that had been pushed against the porch. Father had to set up a ladder and carry him down.

Our pet became naughtier every day. He annoyed the cats and would give our long-suffering collie no peace. The final straw came when an irate feed salesperson found him atop his scratched car.

"That settles it," Father declared. "That nuisance is going to the pasture tomorrow."

Mother gave a sigh of relief.

But Little Barbados was not happy in the pasture. He escaped at least a dozen times, only to be put back again. Gradually he became more contented associating with his own kind, especially when he realized that the other lambs were beginning to imitate his antics. He grew along with the rest and soon developed the curved horns so characteristic of his breed.

Market time arrived, and it was Father's intention to ship him away with the others. But my little sister, Elizabeth, cried so hard that Father changed his mind.

"Well," he conceded gruffly, "I suppose we can keep him till spring. Maybe we can fatten him up a little."

But as it turned out, he stayed forever. Here's how it happened.

My friend Jason and I always took turns driving to our Thursday night youth meeting at church. On this particular evening it was Jason's turn to drive. He lived on the farm that adjoined ours at the top of a hill a half mile down the road. I finished my evening chores and dressed quickly for the meeting. When I tried to call Jason, the phone was completely dead. It was then that my eyes fell on my skis standing against the porch wall.

I glanced at the clock. Only 5:30. That gave me plenty of time to climb the hill and ski down the other side to my friend's home. Mother and my sisters were out feeding the ducks, and I was so impatient to get started that I disobeyed my parents by not telling them what I planned to do. "Always keep us informed of your plans," Mother had often said. "A family should always know where its members are."

Snowflakes were beginning to fall when I carried my skis to the sheep fence, crawled through, and proceeded to the top of the hill. A cold wind was rising, but that didn't deter me. I gloried in the sting of sleet on my face. At the summit I climbed the fence into our neighbor's pasture and strapped on my skis.

Unknown to me, Pastor Jack had canceled the meeting because of the bad weather. He had notified everyone by phone but had been unable to reach me. Naturally he assumed that since Jason and I always came to the youth meeting together, I would find out about it when I arrived at Jason's house.

And I probably would have, except that one of my skis suddenly struck a protruding rock and sent me sprawling. A sharp pain shot through my ankle. I tried to stand but found that I couldn't; the pain was too severe.

"Help, help!" I screamed into the wind. But it only absorbed the sound of my voice and mocked me with its howling.

As I lay there the temperature began dropping, and the cold bit into my body like an icy knife. I screamed for help again and again as the hopelessness of my situation overwhelmed me. I would freeze to death before anyone found me!

"Dear God," I prayed, "send Your holy angel!"

And then, in answer to my prayer, something white appeared out of the darkening shadows. No, it wasn't an angel. It was Little Barbados.

Clearly, he had no notion of my predicament. He butted me playfully a few times. A desperate thought flashed through my mind. If I could keep Little Barbados with me, certainly my folks would miss him when they closed the sheep shed for the night. They'd come looking for him and would get within shouting distance. I encircled his neck with my arms and tried to hold him. It was no use. He pulled away and started toward home.

"Little Barbados, Little Barbados," I coaxed, and he came trotting back. I reached in my pocket to make him think I had a sugar lump. He nuzzled my hand as I pulled out my red bandanna handkerchief. I quickly tied it securely on his horns. Then he left me again.

The evening grew colder and colder. I was lapsing into unconsciousness when I heard Father's anxious voice talking to the sheep.

Barbados answered him with a loud "baa." He was still in the neighbor's pasture. When Father found him at the fence and saw the bandanna tied on his horns, he guessed that I was in serious trouble. Sensing that something was wrong, Barbados led him directly to me.

Father lifted me in his arms and began carrying me down the hill. As he neared the house, he shouted for help. Jason and his father came running. They put me in Jason's bed and called the doctor. Barbados followed us into the house and made himself at home in the bedroom beside me until someone took him to the barn.

All through the night I slipped in and out of consciousness as I shivered and shook uncontrollably. In my dreams I wandered in an endless wasteland of white. An angel walked beside me, but when I looked again, it was Little Barbados. At dawn the doctor pronounced me out of danger.

"Stay in bed for at least a week," he ordered. "You've had a very close brush with death."

Little Barbados lived with us for many years after that. He delighted in each spring's new crop of lambs and was always their leader and playmate. In his fourteenth year he began to fail, so I made a special pen in the barn for him and warmed his water and feed.

The end came peacefully one January morning. We mourned him as one of the family and made a grave up on the hill in the sheep pasture. A pile of stones marks his resting place. To this day, when anyone inquires about those stones, I tell them the story of Little Barbados, the sheep God sent through the snowstorm to save my life.

15

Sammy and the Bear

by Mildred Thompson Olson

The door banged open, and a man, eyes bulging, burst into the room. "I-I just saw a huge bear rippin' blackberries off a bush near the road," he panted. "I froze in my tracks till he went on eatin'; then I ran for my life!" The frightened man stopped and caught his breath. "May I stay here for tonight?"

The farmers who had gathered in the Midway Café erupted into a volcano of noise, everyone talking at once.

"Probably the same bear that killed and ate 10 of my best hens," one farmer insisted.

"Yup, and somethin' got my twin lambs the other night. Probably him!" another added.

"Mr. Hanna told me that something snatched a newborn calf and dragged it down the mountain. Must have been that bear!" added a third.

Eight-year-old Sammy sat unnoticed in the corner, watching the men eat his mother's sugar cookies. He gulped as he imagined that the bear was practically at their doorstep. He wondered what his brother, George, was thinking now. Just yesterday he'd teased Sammy, "Better be good, Sammy, or the bear will come right in here and get you!" Then George had laughed a brave laugh.

Well, he noticed that George wasn't laughing now. George was behind the counter helping Father serve the customers. Sammy watched as George, after shifting uneasily from one elbow to the next, went over and pulled the wooden door shut, latching it.

Aha! Sammy thought. *George is afraid, and tomorrow I'll make him admit it.*

Mother came out of the bedroom that was connected to the back of the café. She slid onto the couch with Sammy and snuggled him in her arms. "Well, your little sister is sound asleep in her trundle bed. Don't you want to go to bed now too?"

Before Sammy could reply, both he and his mother nearly jumped out of their skins when Mr. Nilan pounded a fist on the counter, shouting, "I tell you, folks, I've had enough of this cursed bear! We've got to rid ourselves of him before he kills something else. Now, here's my plan. If any one of us sees him, fire two shots in the air. Then the rest of us will converge on the area where the shots came from and chase him down."

There was a rumble of agreement among the men before they dispersed and went to their homes. Father closed the door behind the last customer and shoved the wooden bolt in place. He turned to the frightened stranger. "We don't run a hotel, friend, just a café. But I wouldn't send you out there for anything. We'll be happy to let you sleep on our old sofa there in the corner. And you're welcome to join our evening devotions."

As Father read the familiar words from Psalm 91, Sammy found some comfort in the promise that God's children needn't be afraid "for the terror by night." After Father's prayer for protection, Sammy should have been able to drop right off to sleep. But he couldn't. He tossed restlessly, his thoughts all mixed up with terrors and bears.

When he heard a noise in the kitchen, he nearly fell off the bed. Then he remembered that his mother was still up, making her special sugar cookies for tomorrow's customers. He could see her easily since his bed was near the door that led into the café. She placed the yummy-smelling cookies on two of the café tables to cool.

Mother soon finished and went to bed. Sammy could tell by the measured breathing that the rest of the family was sleeping soundly. Just as he started to doze off, he thought he heard scratching at the door.

He turned in his bed and stared at the café entrance. He saw nothing, but felt instinctively that something fearful was about to happen.

"Father!" he choked in a hoarse whisper. "Th- there's something at the door!"

"It's probably just the stranger turning on the old couch in the café. Go back to sleep, Sammy," Father mumbled.

Suddenly a loud crunch forced the door open. There, silhouetted in the doorway, was a dark shaggy creature. It was the bear! Sammy froze in his bed. He couldn't talk; he dared not breathe. He watched in terror as the bear ambled out of sight in the direction of the couch.

A few moments later he saw the bear pad over to the table where Mother's sugar cookies were cooling. Sammy watched the bear gulp down the cookies by twos and threes. Then, standing on his hind legs, the bear lifted his paw and swiped the rest of the cookies onto the floor and dropped down to lick up the pieces.

Sammy wanted to scream, but he couldn't. His chest ached for air.

The bear swung his mass around and lumbered into the bedroom. He paused by George's bed, sniffed, and snagged a quilt off the bed. George never stirred, but by now Sammy was trembling uncontrollably as cold chills rippled down his spine. The bear moved to baby Ella's low bed. Dropping George's quilt, he sniffed long and loud. Then he picked Ella up in his huge mouth and scrambled for the door, dropping her pillow on the way.

As the bear trotted out of the café, Ella awakened and cried, "Help me, Mommy!"

Sammy had to do something now! "Please, Jesus," he prayed, "help me; make me talk." He gasped for air. "Father, George, wake up! The bear just took Ella!"

Father landed in the middle of the floor, wide-awake. "What are you saying, son?"

"The bear took Ella," Sammy wailed. "Hurry, Father, before he eats her!"

Moonlight flooding through the open doorway revealed that Ella's bed was indeed empty. Father pulled on his trousers and snatched his gun from the wall. As soon as he was outside, he fired two shots into the air. George and the traveler threw on their clothes and scrambled about for clubs while Mother lit lanterns.

The men charged down the mountain path, following the sound of the bear crashing through the brush. In moments, the voices of neighbors could be heard as they joined in the chase down the steep trail. Shots rang out as men fired at the bear, not realizing that he had Ella.

Finally Sammy roused himself from his stupor and slipped into his clothes. As he laced up his shoes, he saw his mother on her knees, pleading with God to save Ella.

Sammy prayed too as he rushed out the door and along the trail. With only the moonlight to guide him, he slipped down the rocky path, gouging the flesh on his hands and scratching his face on the rough bushes. He could hear the men far below him and knew he'd never catch them. In frustration he stopped and prayed aloud, "Oh, Jesus, please save Ella. Don't let the bear kill her!"

"Sammy!"

Sammy stood rigidly still. Had someone called his name?

"Sammy!" The voice was louder this time.

Was his mind playing tricks on him? "Ella, is that you?" Sammy's voice quivered.

"Sammy, come get me," a plaintive little voice called from the bushes.

Sammy crawled under the shrubs in the direction of his sister's voice. He grasped a bundle. It was her blanket. He crawled farther off the trail, Ella directing him with her cries. He finally reached the little girl and gathered her in his arms. Ella fastened her chubby arms so tightly about his neck that she nearly choked him. But Sammy didn't care!

"I want Mommy!" the little girl pleaded. "Bad bear hurt Ella. See my owies?"

Sammy couldn't see Ella's "owies" under the bushes, but he could get her to Mother. He launched her onto his back and scrambled back up the trail.

Carrying his sister piggyback to the café nearly exhausted the 8-year-old boy, but he hardly noticed.

"I've got her, Mom. I've got Ella!" Sammy called as he stumbled through the door.

Mother hurried from the bedroom and gathered Ella into her arms. "Oh, Ella, my baby, I'm so glad God saved you," Mother repeated again and again as she hugged her daughter. She finally remembered to ring the large dinner bell to signal the men that the lost child had been found.

Gradually the search party drifted into the café and gathered around the little live parcel that the bear had evidently dropped in fright when he heard the first shots from Father's gun. Before the men left the café that night, they knelt on the floor as Father thanked God for the miraculous delivery of his daughter. Then all the men said "amen" and left quietly, giving Sammy a pat on the back for his part in the rescue.

The bear was never seen again. But many years later Ella delighted in telling her grandchildren the story of Sammy and the bear. She even had the bear's teeth mark scars on her arm to prove that "God delivered Daniel from the lions' den, but He delivered me from a bear!"

16

Attack of the Alligator Lithard

by Lori Peckham

My heart pounded as I rang the doorbell for my first babysitting assignment. I hoped that the Wilson kids were nice, and that maybe the parents would give me a few tips for babysitting success.

Unfortunately, the Wilsons were running late. So when the huge wooden door creaked open, Mr. and Mrs. Wilson dashed out, leaving a boy glaring at me.

"Who are you?" he demanded.

"I'm Lori, your babysitter," I smiled. "What's your name?"

The boy squinted. "Rocky."

A little girl took my hand and led me inside. "He's Juthin," the girl lisped, showing a mouthful of peanut butter and red jelly. "I'm Kellie."

"It's *Justin!*" the boy shot at his sister. "Say it

right, or I'll have Bloodbreath bite the rest of your tongue off!"

"Ahhhggg!" the little girl screamed. She rushed toward me and threw her arms around my waist, wiping dirty fingers all over my blouse.

"Uh, who's Bloodbreath?" I ventured, swallowing hard.

Justin exhaled. "You've gotta babysit him, too, so you better meet him. Follow me." He headed down the hall.

I hesitated, then felt Kellie's cold, sticky hand slip into mine. Slowly we followed Justin down the dark hall.

"Isn't there a hall light?" I asked in a whisper.

"It's burned out," Justin responded. He stopped outside a closed door—the last door at the end of the hall.

I could feel my heart pounding. I looked at the signs on the door. One said "Dead End." Another said "Attack Dog," but someone had crossed out the word "dog" and scrawled on "reptile."

"Attack reptile?" I muttered.

Suddenly Justin flung open the door. As it swung back, it struck the wall with a bang.

I let out a gasp and jumped. So did Kellie.

"Bloodbreath can sense your fear," Justin warned. "His species preys on weak, frightened victims."

I let out a breath and crossed my arms. *If there*

really were something dangerous in here, the Wilsons would have told me, I reasoned. *They wouldn't just leave me here totally unprepared. Justin's probably playing a big pretend game. There probably isn't anything in the glass cage he's pointing to.*

"Don't you have a light in here, either?" I asked impatiently, my voice loud in the still room.

Justin advanced toward the glass. "He might be sleeping. You'll have to meet him like this."

A low night-light cast a glow on the beige carpet beneath our feet. Edging closer to the cage, I squinted and peered into the glass. Something moved.

"It's an alligator!" I gasped.

"An alligator lithard," Kellie corrected. "Juthin theths he bithes."

I stared at the sharp, white teeth hanging out of the uneven reptile mouth. The scaly creature began to move around in the small pool of water in the bottom of the cage.

"He senses your fear," Justin said. "He'll eat one of your fingers if I let him out of the cage right now."

"Come on, what does he *really* eat?" I asked, a bit uneasy.

"Anything alive. He's carnivorous."

I looked at Justin skeptically. "Does he really bite?"

"Only people he's never seen before." Suddenly Justin switched the subject. "Hey, *Creature Feature's* on tonight!"

"Ahhhggg!" Kellie screamed. "I hate that thow!"

"What's *Creature Feature?*" I demanded, following Justin into the family room.

"My favorite show." He grabbed the remote control and flipped on the TV.

I hesitated, then sat on the edge of the couch. Kellie plopped down and wrapped her arms around me, nearly cutting off my oxygen supply.

Scary music came from the speakers. Suddenly killer ants, tarantulas, slimy monsters, and one-eyed blobs moved across the screen. Grabbing a pillow, I covered my eyes.

Wait! I thought. *I'm the babysitter here. The Wilsons left me in charge!* I sat up and straightened my shoulders.

"Justin, please change the channel." I wondered how that came across. I wasn't used to telling people what to do.

"Shhh," Justin responded. "I'm trying to watch."

"That's the problem," I said, my confidence growing. "I'm being paid to watch you, and we're not watching this show. Now give me the remote control."

"But I *always* run the remote control," Justin insisted.

"Hand it over," I stated. I even got the courage to stand up and walk over to Justin.

"You get it from me!" he snickered, jumping up and dashing from the room.

The chase was on. Reaching the front door, Justin positioned himself like a skateboarder and slid across the tile in his stocking feet. I followed him and did some sliding of my own—on my behind.

Justin cackled and kept running. Getting up, I followed him down the dark hall. As I neared the sign-decorated door, I heard Justin rummaging around inside.

"Open the door!" I demanded, sliding my hand around the doorknob. It was locked. "Come out here right now!"

Suddenly the door flung open and Justin brushed past me, placing something on my shoulder. Right there, an inch from my nose, the alligator lizard was opening his jaws! The white fangs glistened. The beady eyes flashed. The lizard flicked his tongue at my face. My blood-curdling scream brought Kellie running from the family room.

"Get this thing off me!" I cried, jumping up and down and hunching my shoulders.

The alligator lizard dug its claws into my sweater and neck. Then I felt it on my ear and crawling up onto my head.

I screamed again. "Get him off *now!*"

Kellie just stood there screaming with me, while Justin laughed and slapped his knee. Finally I stopped screaming long enough to get near the bed and sweep the reptile onto the sheets. Still shuddering, I felt my hair and the side of my face for blood. I then dashed into the hall bathroom, locking the door behind me.

"I can't believe how this night is going!" I cried, looking in the mirror, then sitting on the edge of the tub. "Dear Lord, please help me. I need courage. Like David with Goliath, and Daniel in the lions' den."

Slowly I remembered how Justin said Bloodbreath sensed fear. I bet Justin sensed fear too. And he was making use of that to his advantage.

I realized that what I had to do was face the situation head-on. I had to take control.

Justin and Kellie were sitting in the hall outside the bathroom. I flung the door open with a bang, and they both jumped. Then Justin dashed toward me and tossed Bloodbreath on me for the second time.

I stifled the urge to cringe and scream. "Excuse me, but would you please remove this pet from my shoulder?" I said in a controlled voice.

"He's going to bite you! He's going to bite your ear off!" Justin screamed.

"No, he only bites people he's never seen before," I corrected. "And we've already met."

Justin looked disappointed. Kellie beamed, clapped her hands together, and cheered.

"Justin, I want you to take this pet off me right now. He has to get some sleep. And you do too. It's bedtime," I announced.

"OK," Justin bargained, "I'll take him off if I can finish watching Creature Feature."

"Tonight's creature feature is over!" I stated as the lizard came off my shoulder.

Justin rolled his eyes and slumped his shoulders. "I thought you'd be scared," he pouted as he slouched away with Bloodbreath.

"Yes, well, you run along to bed," I commanded.

The rest of the evening went pretty well. God had given me the help and courage I'd asked for. Still, I was certain I felt something crawling on my neck a couple of times.

17

No Fear

by Michael Warren

As we paddled up the twists and turns of the Withlacoochee River, we didn't know what to expect. Early in the morning we had canoed past a large alligator not five feet away from us. When we had approached, it had silently disappeared into the inky black water.

Now suddenly the forest exploded with sound as something crashed through the trees overhead. Wild turkeys! For a city boy like me, it was an astonishing sight. I didn't even realize turkeys could fly. (But they certainly don't fly well, to judge by these ones.)

The fallen trees near the banks were covered with turtles of every size. Some logs were so crowded that the turtles were stacked on top of each other. They always remained still until we were just a few feet away; then they'd scatter and splash into the water.

All except for one tiny Florida cooter. This turtle

was not much bigger than a 50-cent piece, and he was sitting on a rock in the middle of the stream. We canoed up to him, and he didn't even notice. In fact, I just reached out and picked him up.

Usually I don't take animals home with me, but we figured that if this turtle was dumb enough to let us pick it up, it would surely be no match for a great blue heron or an alligator.

We named the turtle Coochee, after the Withlacoochee River where we found him. At home we fixed up a two-gallon aquarium with gravel, rocks, water, and a small plastic tree for shade. We put the tank in our garden window, just above the kitchen sink. Every morning the sunshine would peek through the window and warm Coochee's new home.

It was January at the time, which is cool here in Florida, but not cold. Nevertheless, Coochee seemed to be hibernating, because he wouldn't touch the turtle food we bought for him. He spent most of the day motionless in the water.

Every day I'd check on him, but he barely seemed to notice me. Until spring, that is. By April he was eating every bit of food we gave him, and he was hungry for more. Every time we walked into the kitchen, he would jump off his stone platform and into the water. He would swim toward us furiously. Apparently, he never realized it was impossible to swim through glass.

Although Coochee didn't have as much personality as a cat or dog, I enjoyed having him around. He always had a silly smile on his face, and neighbors and friends loved to see him.

Now that he was eating regularly, Coochee had plenty of energy. He was constantly swimming, but of course he never got anywhere. And now that he was eating regularly, he also began to grow. Soon we realized that we would have to let him go.

A week later we took Coochee with us on a hike out to a prairie where there was a large lake. Many turtles live on this lake, including snappers, musk turtles, and, of course, cooters.

It was a bright, clear day when we set Coochee free. I admit that it was a little difficult to let him go since I had grown attached to him. But what made it even harder was this: as we hiked around the lake, we counted more than 40 alligators.

Even as I let Coochee swim free through the lily pads, I knew that he might not last long in such a difficult environment. Herons, hawks, owls, alligators— I'm sure any of them would be happy to munch on a bite-sized turtle like Coochee.

It may sound odd or a little sentimental, but as I let him go and walked back across the prairie, I said a short and silent prayer, asking God to look after Coochee.

In a way, I guess my prayer was foolish. I know that God looks after every living thing, and that includes turtles. Everything that lives and breathes is alive because God wants it that way. Apart from God, nothing would exist: "For in him we live and move and have our being" (Acts 17:28).

The God who created life also sustains that life and watches over it carefully. And nothing happens to any of God's creatures—especially us—that does not work toward a great purpose (see Romans 8:28).

As the sun began to set on the prairie that afternoon, I began to reflect on my own life. I don't swim with alligators, but I do live in a world that is sometimes dangerous and unpredictable. I'm not always in control of all the circumstances of my world—and neither are the people around me whom I love. This can be a scary thought at times.

But God promises us that there is no reason to be afraid if we trust Him. Nothing escapes God's attention. Jesus said that not even a little bird can fall from its nest without God noticing (see Matthew 10:29).

If God is that concerned about small animals, imagine how much He cares for you! God knows exactly how many hairs are on your head—even after you wash a few down the drain! Jesus reminded us that God is in control: "So don't be afraid" (verse 31).

I don't know what happened to Coochee, but God knows and God cares. Now every time I hike out to that lake, I will think about my pet turtle. And I will remember that God watches over the animals that He made. But far more than that—God watches over you and me.

18

Trapped at Baboon Rock

by Gregory Wessels

Hey, Owen, did you hear that? Sounded like baboons barking," Dave observed as he tightened the last rope securing their tent. He and his friend were camping out in the woods in South Africa.

"Yes, I heard it," Owen responded. "It sounded rather close. Do you suppose they already know we're here?"

"Maybe."

"Dave, would you mind gathering more firewood before it gets too dark for us to see? I'll start a fire using what we already have on hand."

"OK. I'll go into that gully," Dave said, pointing. "I should find plenty of dry wood down there."

The gully was narrow and deep, and large boulders lay strewn about. There was also plenty of dry pine wood, perfect for keeping the two teens' campfire alive.

As Owen stirred the camp stew he was making, he noticed that the sun had set behind Baboon Rock. He knew that the gully had become too dark for Dave to see firewood. *What's taking him so long?* he wondered.

"Dave," Owen shouted, "the stew is simmering in the pot, and the fritters are frying in the pan! Hurry up—I'm starving!"

He heard no answer. He sat on a stone, staring at the fire and listening to the night sounds. Normally, darkness didn't bother him. But with Dave gone, he grew uneasy.

Suddenly Owen froze. He could hear the ominous bark of baboons. Owen knew this meant that a leopard was on the prowl. An owl hooted in a nearby tree as he stoked the fire with the last piece of wood.

Something must have happened to Dave, Owen thought. *He would never stay in the gully after dark. I need to look for him, but there's no way I'm going into that dark gully. Dave will just have to be OK.* His thoughts were in a dreadful turmoil as he picked up the spoon and briskly stirred the stew again.

"Dave, hurry up!" Owen shouted desperately. Staring into the glowing embers, he felt hot tears roll down his cheeks.

Just then a bloodcurdling roar from the gully drove icy spikes of fear through Owen's heart. Grabbing a long, thick stick, he jabbed one end into the fire and waited impatiently as it caught fire. Pulling it out, he reached for his flashlight with his other hand and ran toward the gully.

"Dave, Dave, are you in here?" Owen called as he shone the flashlight beam carefully from boulder to boulder.

Owen cautiously worked his way up the gully, the burning brand in one hand and the flashlight in the other. Then, looking up, he saw a leopard lying on an overhanging branch not six feet above his head! The teenager froze. Backing away ever so slowly, he softly called his friend's name.

"Dave, Dave, where are you?"

"Over here, Owen. Move to your left" came Dave's faint response.

"Keep talking, Dave. Your voice will guide me to you," Owen said. He moved slowly in the direction of Dave's voice while keeping his eyes riveted on the leopard twitching its tail back and forth.

Suddenly Owen stumbled and dropped his flashlight. Searching for it by the eerie light of his flaming torch, he stumbled over his camping mate.

Dave had stepped into a crevasse, and his boot was stuck. Owen noticed that Dave's leg was bleeding badly. *Maybe it's broken*, he thought to himself as he looked into the pale, frightened face of his friend.

"Sorry, Owen," Dave said. "I really messed up this time."

"Don't worry, Dave. I'll think of something in a minute," Owen responded.

Suddenly an earsplitting roar shattered the night. Owen looked up just as the leopard plunged from its perch onto the rocks below.

With a primeval scream that rose from somewhere deep inside him, Owen propelled himself up the path toward the leopard, slashing the darkness with his fiery brand. The startled animal stood its ground for just a moment and then bounded into the darkness of the night.

Crouching beside his friend, Owen peered into Dave's terrified face. "It's OK," he said softly. "He'll be gone for a while."

Owen felt the bones in Dave's leg, thankful that he had learned first-aid techniques. Dave's leg wasn't broken, but it was cut badly. He yanked hard at the rocks that held Dave prisoner. But no matter how hard he pulled and twisted, he couldn't free Dave's boot.

Sweat streamed down Owen's face. His shirt was drenched, his hands bleeding. He was tired and had to rest.

"We're in a horrible mess, aren't we, Owen?"

"I guess so," Owen replied, aware that the leopard would probably return very soon.

"Owen, do you think God would help us if we asked Him?"

"I don't know whether God is interested in this

sort of stuff, Dave, but I think we'd better ask Him anyway." Owen bowed his head. "God," he prayed, "Dave's foot is stuck, and he's hurt bad. I've tried real hard to free him, but it's no use. The leopard is sure to be back soon. We could really use some help. Thank You for listening."

Owen lifted his head and spoke to Dave. "OK, let's try it again."

Owen pulled and pulled with all his might. Suddenly he felt the rock move, and Dave pulled his foot free.

"Thanks, Owen," Dave said to his rescuer.

Helping Dave to his feet, Owen smiled. "Say, I'm ready for some stew. How about you?"

19

Out on a Limb

by Hurl Bates

I t was a cold December day in Oklahoma. I was patrolling Interstate 35 from Oklahoma City south toward Pauls Valley, just south of Purcell. I'd been on duty about four hours, and this had been an uneventful day. Suddenly my radio came to life.

"Headquarters to Unit 41," the dispatcher said.

"Go ahead; Unit 41 here."

"Unit 41, we have a complaint that originates from the McClain farm out on Highway 31. The complaint is a little unclear, but there seems to be an act of cattle rustling, and it's believed to be in progress at this time. Would you confirm this and advise?"

"Ten-four," I responded, then turned on the roof lights on my police cruiser.

At the McClain farm I parked my cruiser and began walking around the nearby rail fence. The fence ran the length of a pasture area with a large barn located at the backside of the field. I looked for anything that might be out of place.

Just then Mrs. McClain came from the main house. At the same moment I noticed something else. About 100 yards from me out in the middle of the pasture grew a giant oak tree. About 20 feet from the ground, out on a limb of the tree, sat a man.

Mrs. McClain drew up beside me, shouting angrily and pointing toward the man in the tree. It appeared that I had stumbled across a scene that I didn't want to play a part in. But my being the law and such, I had a job to do.

"Mrs. McClain," I said in as calm a voice as I could muster, "what's going on here?"

"I'll tell you what's going on," Mrs. McClain said angrily. "That man is trying to steal our bull!"

I could see Mrs. McClain, and I could see the man in the tree. What I didn't see was a bull, nor any way for the man to haul the beast away. Other than my cruiser, there was no vehicle in sight.

By now I knew that the best thing to do was to try to get the whole story. That meant I had to talk to the fellow in the tree. He was looking more shaky by the minute. Walking about halfway out in the pasture, I cupped my hands and yelled at the top of my lungs. "Come on down here; I have some questions that you need to answer."

But the man was not to be persuaded. "I'm not about to come down out of this tree," he shouted back. "You want to talk to me? Well, you're gonna have to come up here or take your chances from there."

"Sir," I called back, "I hate to burst your bubble, but you are coming out of that tree even if I have to come up there and pull you out."

"Suit yourself," the fellow called back. "But if I were you, I'd be headin' back across that fence in a hurry!"

You asked for it, I thought. I could see that he didn't have a weapon, so I took off my service belt, revolver and all, and placed it gently on the ground.

Big mistake.

I heard the noise before I saw it, and then my attention was drawn across the field and to the left of the tree. Right there my eyes beheld one of the meanest and biggest bulls I had ever had the misfortune of meeting, and he was coming my way! Fact is, he would have made the Indianapolis 500 cars look slow by comparison. It looked to me as if fire was coming out of his nostrils and smoke was coming from his feet.

Now, I've been through earthquakes, tornadoes, and fires. I weigh about 210 pounds, and I've never run from anything in my life. But right then I said a quick prayer and scooted up that tree. My service revolver still lay on the ground right where I had placed it.

Being up the creek without a paddle doesn't hold a candle to being up a tree with a big bad bull beneath you that would just love to mess up your day.

Right next to me sat the man I had come to get out of the tree.

"I tried to warn you not to come up here," he said. "I've been up here almost two hours, and this snow and wind sure aren't doing much to brighten my day." He went on to say, "Last night I talked to Fred McClain over at the auction in Lexington. He wanted me to come over here today and look at this bull. Fred said the bull was gettin' to be a menace around the farm. And since I've been trying to find a bull, he said I should make him an offer on this one. Wasn't no one around when I got here, so I parked my car over behind the main house."

Now, if you think our little problem couldn't have gotten worse, then you would surely be wrong. While walking around the tree, the bull had spotted my service belt lying on the ground. He walked over to it, grabbed it in his mouth, and tossed it into the air. As it would happen, when it was coming down, it caught smack around the horns of that bull.

At first we'd had us an agitated bull, but now we had an agitated bull with a gun!

Just then I spotted Mrs. McClain strolling out of the barn carrying a bucket in her hand. She patted the side of the feed bucket as she crossed the fence and walked slowly toward us.

I can now say that I have never seen a more beautiful sight than Mrs. McClain at that moment. The bull seemed to lose all his anger and calmly followed Mrs. McClain—and her feed bucket—into the barn. In the process, my service belt and revolver dropped into the snow-covered muck.

Well, I came out of this adventure with nothing much hurt except my pride. I did learn two very important lessons that day, though. First, don't get caught downwind of a big mean bull. Second, things aren't always what they appear to be at first sight. It's a lesson Christians especially ought to learn. I do believe Mrs. McClain and we two men learned that lesson real well.

20

The Forbidden Shed

by Patti Emanuele

I watched the two lizards climbing my bedroom wall. One was named Harold; the smaller one was Fern. I was used to seeing them every morning.

The rhythmic pounding outside my window had awakened me. It would continue for several more hours. Every day the strong African women living on our compound arose before daybreak to pound boiled yams into the day's meal.

I knew Maryamma would be there instructing the younger brides to pound harder. She was kind and gentle to me. Many times her thick brown fingers would brush my blond hair back from my face as she remarked, "Little one, blue eyes cannot see." I loved her.

With three years of missionary experience, my parents had finally made this home. Our compound, modest and obscure, sat at the edge of the Sahara.

This morning I eagerly pushed the mosquito netting back from my bed. Anwar and I were going to investigate the shed for puppies. We had seen a wild dog crawl into the shed yesterday, her belly heavy with young.

I tried to block out Father's warning. "Stay away from her," he had said. "She might have rabies."

Bouncing out of bed, I searched for my dress. I could hear my mother tending to the baby, Christina. I knew that her crib was also covered with mosquito netting in an attempt to ward off dreaded malaria.

"Honey," my mother said when I appeared in the kitchen, "didn't you wear that dress yesterday?" My mother never misses anything.

I slipped into a seat at the kitchen table, choosing to ignore the question. In front of me lay breakfast: sliced French bread, jam, and a glass of milk. All our milk had to be boiled because of the threat of tuberculosis.

My mother struggled to put Christina into the rickety high chair. Without asking I knew that my father was long gone to visit the farmers.

At the sound of Anwar's greeting I turned and saw my friend at our open door. Being adventurous and mischievous, we enjoyed each other's company.

"Come on," he whispered, tugging at my arm. "Let's go."

Eager to be free from the kitchen, I gulped down

the rest of the milk and pointed it out to my mother. "See, all done." She smiled at me and then became distracted by her many chores.

"Good morning, little ones," the men greeted as they passed us on their path to work in the fields.

The shed was at the far end of the compound. Farm equipment was stored there, and we were generally warned to "stay out of there—it's dangerous." Everyone was busy enough today that we would be able to slip inside unnoticed.

The promise of newborn puppies quelled my uneasiness about entering the semi-dark room. I had lived in Africa long enough to know that entering anything in the dark was not a good idea. But puppies are harmless, and they certainly would be fun.

Anwar led the way, and I carefully held on to the tail of his shirt. "Shhh," he said when I began to speak.

There were only two windows in the large building. Sunlight streamed through them, illuminating the front of the room. As we continued toward the back, the darkness became deeper.

"Anwar," I said again.

Now his voice was impatient. "Quiet; we don't want to wake the mother dog," he whispered.

The very back of the shed held the larger equipment. There was a tractor in need of repair, and various shovels and rakes lay scattered upon the dirt floor. Anwar suddenly stopped, and I bumped into him. He tried unsuccessfully to suppress a chuckle.

We heard a rustle in the darkness, and Anwar pointed toward the old tractor. He moved closer. I began to feel uncomfortable and clutched his arm. Why didn't the puppies make a sound?

"There," he breathed. "Over there." He stepped up to where the rusty tractor lay spread against the wall. Then I heard him scream.

"Run," he said. "Run!"

I turned and stumbled toward the door. As daylight began to spread across my path, I saw what was chasing us. We had stumbled upon a nest of baby vipers. Their bite was certain death, since there was no antivenin.

The aggressive creatures were known to chase their victims until they caught them. The Africans feared them and would much rather encounter a cobra. A nest of viper snakes meant a threat to the entire compound, and certain death to babies and children.

We burst through the shed doors, small wiggling bodies chasing us into the sandy yard.

"Snakes!" we screamed.

Garba, the farm manager, ran toward us with a machete in his hand. He slashed away at our pursuers.

That evening my father and I had a talk, and I said I was sorry. I knew that by not listening to my father I had placed Anwar and myself in danger. After the expected lecture, my father assigned me several tasks. The last one on the list was to go down and clean out the cow barn.

Reluctantly I obeyed, knowing that it was my fault that I was in trouble. When I arrived at the cow barn, the stalls were surprisingly clean.

"Now what am I supposed to do?" I grumbled to our cow that was calmly chewing her feed.

I gasped in delight as I saw, just beyond her, a mother dog and her babies curled up in the corner.

21

Miracle in Nigeria

by Roger W. Coon

Twelve-year-old Sally lived with her missionary parents at a Baptist mission station in the northern part of Nigeria. Friends told Sally's family about an interesting feature that they had recently watched on the new national television network. In the program, two American Seventh-day Adventist missionaries in southern Nigeria appeared with their Chihuahua, which had fathered puppies. These little puppies were believed to have been the first of this breed of dog ever to be born in all of Nigeria, Africa's most populous nation.

There were three tiny puppies in the litter. And since Chihuahuas are very small—even when fully grown—these three newly born puppies could easily be held in the joined palms of two cupped hands. How adorable they were!

Upon hearing of this story, Sally had a bright idea. She herself owned a little white female Chihuahua named Tina. "Why don't we arrange for Tina to have puppies with the Chihuahua we saw on TV?" she suggested to her parents. "That way I'd have some puppies to play with!"

Through the help of an American Baptist missionary dentist living at Ibadan (Africa's largest native city) in southern Nigeria, arrangements were made with the Adventist missionaries to breed the dogs on the campus of the Adventist Seminary of West Africa (now Babcock University).

Another Baptist missionary family, traveling down to the coast at about this same time, agreed to act as go-betweens and take Sally's dog with them to the Adventist compound, about 500 miles to the south.

At noon on their trip down, the missionary's wife said, "Why don't we pull over and have a bite to eat?" The family stopped by the side of the jungle road in a very desolate, largely uninhabited area between the old walled city of Kaduna and the great Niger River.

While their car was stopped, Sally's little white dog slipped unnoticed out through an open back door. Finished with their meal, the travelers resumed their journey and were many miles down the road when the missionary's wife blurted out, "The dog is gone!" But it was far too late to turn back. Besides, it was most unlikely, had they decided to retrace their steps, that they would have found the little dog still there on the jungle road.

Upon learning this disappointing news, Sally was heartbroken that her beloved Tina was lost somewhere in the African jungle. But she prayed fervently for the return of her pet. And with unshakable faith Sally assured anyone willing to listen that God would surely bring her dog back to her. "Don't worry!" she would always add cheerfully.

Meanwhile, Roger and Irene Coon, the Adventist missionaries who were expecting the arrival of Sally's dog for breeding, began to wonder why it had never shown up at their home. What could be the delay? Finally they learned the whole sad story.

But the little white Chihuahua was on an incredible adventure of her own.

A short time after Tina had slipped out of the car, a British couple came driving down the same road. The wife, idly looking out the car window, suddenly gasped in astonishment. "Dear," she said to her husband, "you just passed a white Chihuahua on my side of the road!"

Her husband laughed at what he thought was a funny joke. "A Chihuahua out here, in this remote, desolate place? That's a pretty good one. Why, there isn't a Chihuahua within 200 miles of this place. No one even lives within 50 miles of here. What would a Chihuahua be doing in a deserted area like this, anyway?"

But the woman stubbornly insisted that she *had* seen a small white Chihuahua by the side of the road. "We must turn back!" she said.

To appease his wife, the man stopped the car, turned around, and drove back in the direction from which they had come, for about a half mile.

Sure enough, there was a little white Chihuahua trotting down the jungle road, unaware of the travelers who were now observing it in disbelief.

The British couple stopped their car and called the dog over to them. Gently picking Tina up, they took the dog with them in their car the rest of the way to their home in Lagos in southern Nigeria.

About this time the Coon family decided to take a one-day excursion away from the seminary where they lived and worked.

"Let's go to the coast," Mrs. Coon suggested. "It's only 50 miles south of here." They had heard of a lovely resort beach called Tarkwa Bay, which was reported to be safe from the treacherous undertow that often swept unwary swimmers out to sea.

The Coons and their two preschool children, Suzie and Donnie, traveled down to the coast and parked their car near a grove of coconut trees. They hired someone to transport them by canoe across the beautiful lagoon.

Upon their arrival on the other side of the lagoon, the family struggled up a large sand dune on the island, trying to manage their picnic basket, thermos jug, blanket, swimsuits, and towels. That's when Mrs. Coon noticed a small white Chihuahua running past them on the crest of the dune.

"Roger!" Mrs. Coon called out. She then told her husband what she'd seen. At the time there probably weren't more than a half dozen Chihuahuas in all of Nigeria. Suddenly Mrs. Coon announced, "I'm going to find out who owns that dog."

That task didn't take long. Greeting the owners—or who she thought were the owners—Mrs. Coon called to them, "We have Chihuahuas too. How long have you had yours?"

"Oh," replied the British woman sitting on the sandy beach, "this dog isn't ours. You'll never believe this, but we found her several weeks ago, trotting down an isolated jungle road halfway between the Niger River and the old walled city of Kaduna up in northern Nigeria, in a very desolate, uninhabited area. So we stopped and picked up the dog. She must have belonged to somebody and was obviously lost."

The woman went on. "When we got home we advertised in the lost-and-found classified section of the Lagos *Daily Times*. But so far no one has responded to our ad, and we're just keeping her until we can find out to whom she belongs."

Mrs. Coon grinned broadly, then said, "Well, I know to whom she belongs. In fact, I believe the dog's name is Tina, as I recall."

Sure enough, at the mention of her name the little dog pricked up her ears and turned to see who was calling her! Mrs. Coon then told the surprised woman the rest of the story. She gave the woman all the information necessary to contact Tina's owners.

It wasn't long before little Tina was reunited with Sally. And everyone who heard the story was astonished at how the whole thing had all worked out— except Sally.

"I'm not surprised," she declared with strong conviction. "I just asked Jesus to bring my Tina back home. And He did. Jesus answered my prayer— what's so unusual about that?"

Well, how about this: What are the mathematical odds of two persons, who had never even met each other before, bumping into each other in Africa's largest nation, on a beach that had been visited by one of them only once in the entire 12 years of her service as an Adventist missionary to that West African nation?

Those odds must have been astronomical! But God is bigger than even the biggest odds.

And if God cares this much about a little missionary dog lost in the heart of tropical Africa, think of the miracles He can perform for the people lost in Africa and everywhere else. And think of what He can do for you.

22

The Bull That Preached

by Rachel Whitaker

Pastor Timothy, I need your advice." Nathaniel's furrowed brow revealed his concern. "The nurses from the Seventh-day Adventist hospital in Atoifi are holding a clinic here in Kwaibaita. You've often warned us about Adventists' misguided doctrines. Is it safe to go to their clinic?"

Pastor Timothy thought carefully before replying. As a pastor and the paramount chief of the entire Kwaibaita district, he was well respected by the people of his community in the Solomon Islands.

"We do need medical care here in the village," he admitted. "You can accept the Adventists' medications, but don't listen to their teachings. If they tell you anything about the Bible or the church, just ignore it."

After Nathaniel left, Pastor Timothy felt a pang

of guilt. *In 20 years as a pastor, I've found some texts in the Bible that make me wonder if the Adventists are right about some things. Take the fourth commandment, for example . . .*

He quickly shoved that thought out of his head. What would his church members think if he suddenly changed his mind about Adventists and their teachings?

"We have a lot of work to do in the garden this morning," Pastor Timothy said to his wife and their 10-year-old son, Bofanta, one September day in 1990. It was a Sabbath morning, but that did not bother Pastor Timothy, since he did not believe that Saturday was the Sabbath. "The taro plot will be full of weeds after all the rain we've had."

The three of them walked down the path away from the village. Pastor Timothy paused to open the gate of the cow pasture they had to cross to reach their garden.

As they neared the other side of the enclosure, his wife spoke up. "Look at how all the cows have lined up facing us. It's almost as if they're trying to block our way."

"They look like soldiers on parade," said Pastor Timothy with a laugh. "I suppose they'll move when we get closer."

But the cows didn't move. *Odd,* he thought. *I guess we'll have to go around them.*

At the end of the line stood a large, muscular bull that seemed to be staring straight at them. As the family approached, the bull suddenly spoke in the Kwaibaita language. "Why are you going to the garden now? Don't you know that today is the seventh day, the Sabbath of the Lord God?"

Pastor Timothy's jaw dropped. "Did you hear that?" he croaked to his wife.

"I—I think the bull just talked!" she whispered hoarsely.

Pastor Timothy looked around, certain that he must have been mistaken. No one else was in sight.

Then he heard the voice again. "Timothy!" His head swiveled toward the bull. "Timothy, I'm speaking to you!"

Yes, the sound was coming from the animal. Its mouth was even moving as it talked.

"Th—there must be a devil in you to make you talk like that," Pastor Timothy said, his voice trembling.

"I am not the devil," the bull replied. "I am the voice of Jesus talking to you."

Pastor Timothy really paid attention then! The bull went on: "Today is the Sabbath of God. Don't you know that God gave you six days to work, and the seventh day is the Sabbath? You have been a pastor, and yet you don't know these things? How blind can you be?"

He's right, Pastor Timothy thought. *I've been re-*

fusing to believe the truth all this time.

But the bull was not finished. "You must not work in your garden today. Go home and read Jeremiah 1:5. Share it with your people. Then look for the Seventh-day Adventist pastor, Pastor Bata. He will further explain these things to you."

Pastor Timothy waited, but the bull said nothing more. The pastor dropped to his knees in the field and began to cry. "I'm supposed to be a spiritual leader," he moaned, "but instead I've been teaching my church members the wrong things! I'm sorry, Lord."

The pastor and his family immediately headed back to their house, taro plants and weeds forgotten.

"I must look up the text the bull mentioned," Pastor Timothy said when they reached home. He found the passage in his Bible and read it aloud: "'Before I formed you in the womb I knew you, before you were born I set you apart; I appointed you as a prophet to the nations.'"

"What does that have to do with the Sabbath?" asked Bofanta.

"I think God is saying that I need to share this message with others," his father replied.

Pastor Timothy called the entire village together and told them what had happened. "It was the voice of Jesus that spoke to me through the bull," he said. "We must not do any work today. We must begin resting on the Sabbath."

The people stared at him in amazement. But they respected their pastor and chief, so everyone in the village kept that Sabbath.

Early the next morning Pastor Timothy set off through the bush toward Atoifi Adventist Hospital. Questions rushed through his mind as he walked along the steep rocky mountain trail. There were so many things he needed to ask the Adventist pastor!

After a four-hour hike through the lush tropical forest, he reached the hospital and approached the first employee he saw.

"My name is Timothy, and I'm the chief of Kwaibaita," he said. "I am looking for Pastor Bata."

"Who told you about Pastor Bata?" the puzzled employee asked.

Pastor Timothy didn't answer the question directly. "I have a story to tell Pastor Bata," he said.

Someone took him to the village where Pastor Bata was working. "I've already kept the Sabbath," Pastor Timothy told him. "I need to know more."

The two pastors studied the Bible together for three months. "I want to be baptized," Pastor Timothy decided. "And I want to do it in my village so that all my people can see the choice I'm making."

Pastor Timothy's baptism was a big event in Kwaibaita. Most of his church members showed up to see the man who had warned them against Adventism become an Adventist himself.

"For many years I taught you things that I knew were not according to the Bible," Pastor Timothy confessed. "I ask your forgiveness for leading you astray."

He looked out over the crowd, full of people he cared about. "I've shared with you many of the things I've learned from the Adventist pastor. I believe them to be the truth. Will you join me in following God's Word? If you will join me, come stand over here to my right. If you want to stay with your current beliefs, stand on my left."

For a moment no one moved. Then several people jumped up and strode purposefully toward Pastor Timothy's right. A few, with looks of horror on their faces, headed in the opposite direction.

As more and more people in the crowd chose one side or the other, Pastor Timothy's face broke into a broad smile. The majority of the villagers were taking their stand with him to follow God's truth!

Soon a new church was built in Kwaibaita where Pastor Timothy and his people could worship God every Sabbath.

And the talking bull? He hasn't said a word since. He doesn't need to. He lets Pastor Timothy do all the preaching about the Sabbath.

Thanks to David Tasker, Jim Manele, and Tadashi Ino for providing the information for this story.